# Violin

## AN EASY GUIDE

# Violin

## AN EASY GUIDE

NEW HOLLAND

**chris coetzee**

First published in 2003 by
New Holland Publishers
London • Cape Town • Sydney • Auckland
www.newhollandpublishers.com

86 Edgware Rd
London W2 2EA
United Kingdom

80 McKenzie Street
Cape Town 8001
South Africa

14 Aquatic Drive
Frenchs Forest, NSW 2086
Australia

218 Lake Road
Northcote, Auckland
New Zealand



ISBN 1 84330 331 0 (HB); 1 84330 332 9 (PB)

Reproduction by Unifoto Pty Ltd
Printed and bound in Malaysia by Times Offset
2 4 6 8 10 9 7 5 3 1

Publisher: Mariëlle Renssen
Publishing manager (SA): Claudia Dos Santos
Publishing manager (UK): Simon Pooley
Commissioning editor: Karyn Richards
Managing art editor: Richard MacArthur
Designer: Peter Bosman
Editor: Sandy Shepherd
Picture researcher: Karla Kik
Production: Myrna Collins
Consultant: Mark Messenger (Head of Strings, Royal College of Music)

## AUTHOR'S DEDICATION

This book is dedicated to my grandfather, who knows half of everything, and my grandmother, who knows the other half. Also to my brother, who suffered most during my practice sessions, and to my teacher, Louis van der Watt, who knows good music when he hears it. Finally, this book is dedicated to all my mentors in music – those who still live and those who have been dead for hundreds of years.

# contents

# WHY PLAY THE VIOLIN?

THIS IS A BOOK FOR ENTHUSIASTS, written by an enthusiastic musician. I do not claim it will teach you to play the violin perfectly, since even the most seasoned players agree the violin is a devil of an instrument to master. It can take years to go from playing spectacularly badly to merely competently. However, the violin has a magic which it weaves over its unsuspecting victims, carrying them through the initial hardships until they find themselves satisfied in ways they did not know were possible. So, take courage. It is not as bad as it sounds.

We live in a technologically driven era, and one in which commercial and financial concerns influence almost all spheres of human activity. It is not surprising, therefore, that more and more people take up a hobby to stimulate the creative part of themselves that has been all but forgotten. A great many want to learn to play a musical instrument. Instruments and lessons are often far from cheap, however, and many books on the subject are incomprehensible to anyone without a musical background. In addition, learning an instrument takes a lot of time and patience, commodities which are seriously lacking in our frenetically paced society. The biggest stumbling block for any beginner, however, is the exclusive attitude that is, unfortunately often, a characteristic of the music industry when dealing with the lay person. Luckily, all these difficulties can easily be overcome or simply ignored.

This book, concise, unpretentious and accessible, tries to make things easy. It gives a brief history of the violin and explains how it makes its sound, describes how to hold the bow and produce different notes, and will also teach you the basics of reading music. I have given various tips on buying an instrument as well as some sheet music, and have suggested a few recordings featuring the violin.

It is important to remember that the violin is quite difficult to learn on your own. So, read this book and, if it inspires you, find a good teacher (see p92) as soon as possible in order to learn how to play properly from the beginning. My aim was to make this book informative and interesting to read so that it will help anyone, no matter what his or her musical background, to discover the thrill and pleasure of making music on the violin.

**OPPOSITE** Whether you are a novice or professional, young or old, playing the violin is a social activity which can provide a great amount of enjoyment.

# THE ORIGINS OF THE VIOLIN

The violin was developed in a time of experimentation in instrument-building and was designed to imitate the human voice. It evolved in the 1490s as a result of the so-called 'consort principle' (an ensemble of similar instruments built in several different sizes to accommodate all the notes of a piece of music, capable of giving a homogeneous sound). From this consort principle emerged the modern violin family as we know it today: violin, viola and cello.

Initially, the violin had three strings, as seen in Italian paintings from the early 1500s. A fourth string was added later, and the 'classic' form of the violin became established by the 1550s. An earlier cousin, the viol, was also made in different sizes, usually with between five and seven strings, and featured frets, like the guitar. The viol is commonly referred to as the viola da gamba (viol on the knees), to distinguish it from the viola da braccia (viol on the arm).

The members of the violin family include (from left to right) the violin, viola and cello.

A violino (renaissance violin) player, from Bonanni's *Gabinetto Armonico*, first printed 1716. The violino appeared in the mid 16th century. Note the unfretted fingerboard.

In its early days, the violin was used principally for dance and ballet music. Its popularity ensured that composers wrote music for it and, by 1600, they began specifying the violin as their instrument of choice.

This increase in popularity was due, in part, to the high standard of violin-making during this time, which, in the 16th and 17th centuries, centred on Italy. Verona and Venice were important in this regard. Later, the cities of Cremona and Brescia became the centres of excellence in violin-making.

Important makers of fine violins include Andrea Amati (*c*1511–77) and his two sons, Antonio (1540–1607) and Girolamo (1561–1630). Among the pupils of Andrea's illustrious grandson Nicolò (1596–1684), who had enormous impact on the future of the instrument, was the famous Antonio Stradivari (*c*1644–1737), whose violins form the basis for most later instruments. This was the first time in history that a 'brand name' became important and Italian violins became all the rage throughout the rest of Europe.

After this, comparatively few changes were made to the design of the violin. When changes were made, it was usually to accommodate the ideal sound of the time. As time progressed, new instruments were made more robust and old instruments were (sacrilegiously) brought 'up to date'. This trend was so important that precious few of the older instruments have come down to us in their original form. The main reason for this was that musicians (especially soloists) of the 19th century wanted an instrument with greater tonal

Virtuoso violinist Niccolò Paganini (1782–1840) was the 19th-century equivalent of a rock star.

power (a grand way of saying louder) and brilliance (a bright, piercing sound). The other reason, of course, was the fact that the concert halls of the 19th century were much larger than earlier ones and therefore had to be filled with sound.

Violin virtuosi (technically brilliant players) like Niccolò Paganini (1782–1840) were considered the 'rock stars' of their day and attracted huge audiences, all of whom wished to hear the violin, even if they were sitting in the back row.

The first strings date from around the 14th century, and were made from sheep's gut, and sometimes silk. These formed the core for metal wound strings, which became standard after 1750. The lower two strings were wound and the upper two were plain gut. Modern wound strings are wound with metal ribbon made from aluminium, silver or gold. In the late 19th century, the highest string became solid metal, but was replaced with synthetic nylon fibres, which were introduced in 1946. Today, most musicians prefer nylon strings, because they are less likely to warp or break. Classical musicians prefer nylon strings, whereas folk musicians prefer metal strings.

The earliest bows were curved, like their precursor, the hunting bow. By 1625, heavier bows were preferred, for crisper articulation (see p36). Over time the shape of the stick was straightened and the bow was lengthened. The modern bow was established in 1785 by François Tourte (1747–1835), which is why it is known as the 'tourte' bow.

Electric amplification became fashionable in the mid-20th century, especially in styles like jazz and blues, often because the music was too loud for the unamplified violin to hold its own. Even though the electric violin has become popular again through artists like Vanessa Mae and the string quartet known as Bond, it has never really found a place in classical music. The sound is much more suited to jazz and pop music. The classical music industry in general is concerned with playing music as the composer might have heard it. Most composers throughout the ages would not know what an electric violin looks like even if you beat them with one.

Singaporean solo violinist Vanessa Mae brought sex appeal and a pop sound to violin-playing, which kindled interest in younger listeners and a wider spectrum of music-lovers.

# THE ANATOMY OF THE VIOLIN AND BOW

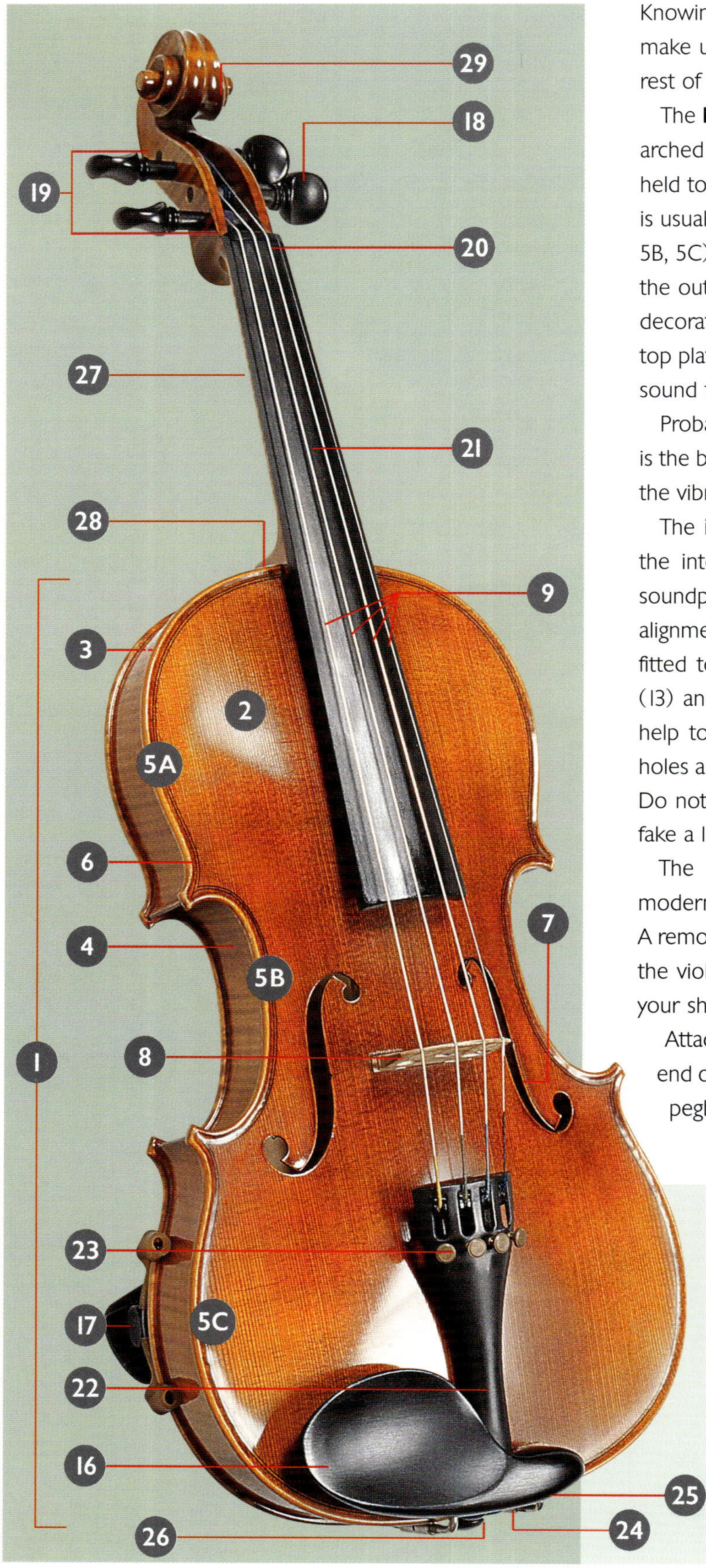


Knowing the names of most of the 70-odd bits and bobs that make up the violin and its bow will help you understand the rest of this book and other books on the subject.

The **body** (1) of the violin (left) is hollow and consists of an arched top plate or belly (2) and an arched back plate (3), held together by the sides, or ribs (4). The shape of the body is usually divided into the upper, middle and lower bouts (5A, 5B, 5C). A curved band, or purfling (6), forms a border along the outer edge of the top and back plates. Apart from being decorative, the purfling stops cracks from spreading. On the top plate are the sound holes or f-holes (7), which permit the sound to escape from the body of the violin.

Probably the most important part of the entire instrument is the bridge (8). It supports the strings (9) and communicates the vibrations (or sound) to the body.

The **inside of the body** (illustrated opposite) contains all the interesting bits you cannot see from the outside. The soundpost (10) and the bass-bar (11) are in approximate alignment with the feet of the bridge. The sound post is lightly fitted to allow maximum conductivity. The top (12), bottom (13) and corner blocks (14), as well as the lining strips (15), help to strengthen the instrument. Peer through the sound holes and you will see the label of the maker or manufacturer. Do not be fooled if it says Stradivarius – it is much easier to fake a label than it is to fake a violin.

The last thing on the body, which is standard on most modern violins, is the chin rest (16), which does what it says. A removable shoulder rest (17; see also p90), helps to balance the violin on your shoulder so that you do not have to pull your shoulder up to keep the violin in place.

Attached to the body of the violin are the four strings. One end of a string is fastened around a tuning peg (18) inside the pegbox (19). The string is stretched over the nut (20) to

1. **body**
2. **top plate/belly**
3. **back plate (unseen)**
4. **sides/ribs**
5. **upper (A), middle (B) and lower (C) bouts**
6. **purfling**
7. **f-holes/sound holes**
8. **bridge**
9. **strings**
10. **soundpost**
11. **bass-bar**
12. **top block**
13. **bottom block**
14. **corner blocks**
15. **lining strips**
16. **chin rest**
17. **shoulder rest**
18. **tuning peg**
19. **peg box**

hold it at the correct height above the fingerboard (21). The string passes over the bridge and the other end is fastened to the tailpiece (22) which usually contains four fine tuners (23). The tailpiece is held against the main body of the violin by means of the tailgut (24) which passes over the saddle (25) and is twisted around the end-button (26). The end-button is attached to the bottom block (inside the body). In the same way the neck (27), which supports the fingerboard, is attached to the top block (also inside the body) at the shoulder (28). At the top of the neck, apart from the pegs and peg box, is the scroll (29). In the past it was made to look like the head of a woman, lion or angel, but these days it is simply a curly bit of wood. It may seem purely ornamental, but it is often used to hang up the violin to allow the varnish to dry.

As important as the violin is the **bow** (right). The wooden part (A) is called the stick (no surprise there). The hairy part the ribbon, or hair (B), is made up of approximately 150 hairs, almost always from the tail of a horse. The top of the bow is called the point (C) and the bottom the frog (D) – the reason for this name is a mystery. At the bottom of the bow is the adjuster, or screw (E), which adjusts the tautness of the ribbon by moving the frog forwards and backwards. The lapping (F), usually made of leather, and the winding (G), usually made from thin metal wire, help to protect the stick since this is the place with which your fingers come into most contact. It also gives you a better grip on the bow.

Something which does not form part of the violin but is essential for it to work properly is **rosin** (H). This semi-transparent substance is made from the gum of trees and comes in blocks, in many shapes and sizes. You rub it against the ribbon of the bow, coating it with a fine powder. When the bow is drawn across the strings, the rosin adhering to the bow hair causes the bow to grip the strings, creating better friction. If it weren't for the rosin, the bow would slide over the strings without producing much sound.

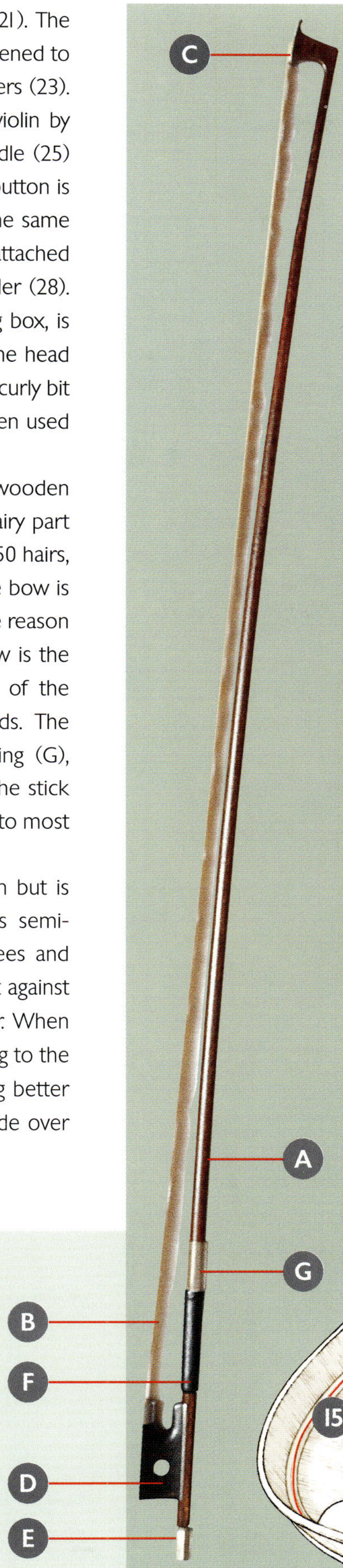

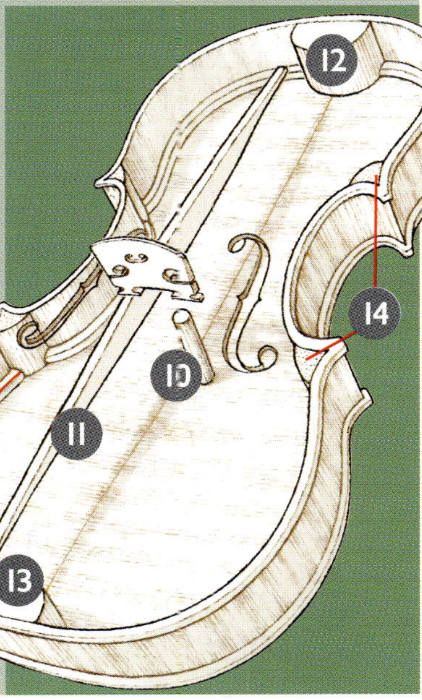


**20. nut**
**21. fingerboard**
**22. tailpiece**
**23. fine tuners**
**24. tailgut**
**25. saddle**
**26. end-button**
**27. neck**
**28. shoulder**
**29. scroll**

**A. stick**
**B. ribbon/hair**
**C. point**
**D. frog**
**E. adjuster/screw**
**F. lapping**
**G. winding**
**H. rosin**

# HOW DOES THE VIOLIN WORK?

The violin is regarded (mostly by violinists) as the most perfect instrument ever created. Essentially, it is nothing more, nor less, than a vibrating wooden box. However, this vibrating wooden box, no bigger than three bottles of wine, can make a very large audience drunk with its sound. This is no mean feat and there is obviously much more to this small instrument than meets the eye.

Since the science behind the sound is linked to how you play the violin I have given a simple explanation of the acoustic principles governing the violin. A firm knowledge of how the violin produces its sound is beneficial to beginner and expert alike, since it gives some insight into the strengths and weaknesses of the instrument.

Sound is nothing more than vibrations in the air. If the vibrations are constant, a stable pitch will result. The frequency of the vibrations, measured in hertz, affects the pitch. The higher the frequency, the higher the resulting note will be; the lower the frequency, the lower the note.

The agents that cause the violin to make a sound are its strings. These strings are 'activated' when you either stroke them with the bow or pluck them with your fingers. Once a string has been activated, a series of things happens which results in a note. The bridge transmits these vibrations to the belly while the soundpost transmits some of the vibrations to the back plate. The belly is made of a soft wood (usually spruce) which vibrates easily and so it functions as the soundboard of the violin. The sound then bounces off the back and sides while the hollow body further amplifies the sound, which then leaves the violin through the sound holes towards the ears of the listener.

It is also important to understand the properties of a vibrating string since they are so intimately bound to the violin's sound production. In order to raise the pitch, you have to make the string vibrate faster. Shortening the so-called 'vibrating length' of the string achieves this. By stopping (pressing down) the string higher up on the fingerboard (closer to the bridge) you shorten the vibrating length and create a higher note. By contrast, an open string (one which is not stopped but allowed to vibrate freely) produces the lowest pitch a specific string can sound.

**TOP RIGHT** An open (unfingered) string produces the lowest possible note for that string.
**BOTTOM RIGHT** Stopping a string shortens the vibrating length and raises the pitch.

There are several other ways that you can influence the speed of the strings' vibrations. Varying the tension of the string is one (the higher the tension, the quicker the vibrations). You do this by tightening or loosening the tuning pegs or fine tuners.

Another way is to increase the string's weight, since a heavier string vibrates more slowly than a light one. For this reason the lower strings are wound with wire. The weight combines with the tension to give the correct pitch for the open note of that specific string.

There are scores of academic and scientific articles dealing with the violin's 'sound zones' and the resonating properties of certain types of varnish (not to mention the grain of the wood and the size and shape of the sound holes). All are worth a read, if this is what floats your boat (or vibrates your string – as it were).

**RIGHT** Varying the tension of the strings is one way of altering the pitch produced by the open string.

The lower strings of the violin are wound with wire to give them extra weight, which makes them vibrate more slowly and produce a deeper sound than the lighter strings.

chapter two

# LEARNING THE LANGUAGE

MUSIC IS THE MOST RIDICULOUSLY EASY LANGUAGE IN THE WORLD. If you know the first seven letters of the English alphabet and can multiply and divide by two, then you are already halfway there. But, like any language, you need a basic grasp of its grammar and vocabulary to communicate effectively. By practising just a few minutes each day, you will be able to read music in a fraction of the time it takes to learn even the most rudimentary English. Of course, it is not possible to cover all aspects of reading music in a few pages, but what has been included here is enough to get you started.

I have explained each musical concept, and a graphic representation is given for visual reference. Western music is written down as a visual representation of what you hear. It started more than a thousand years ago in the cloisters and cathedrals of medieval Europe, where the church service was sung or chanted by the clergy and assisted by the choir. As the liturgy expanded, however, it became impossible to remember all the tunes. The clergy started experimenting with different ways of reminding the choir of the melody, including hand signals and musical notation (the dots and squiggles on the page). The words of a hymn were written down with little squiggly markings above them, ascending and descending as the melody did. But this was very imprecise, because it did not show on which note the choir should begin, and soon a single line was added to the notation to solve the confusion. Any notes written on the line were sung on a specific note, while anything written above the line was sung higher and anything below it was sung lower. A second line was added later, which narrowed down the number of possible notes between the two lines. More and more lines were added, and by the late 16th century, there were the five lines that constitute the modern musical 'stave' (see p23). The squiggles also underwent various changes in order to describe the rhythm of the melody more accurately, and so our modern 'notes' were born.

Music notation soon became an international language. Musicians throughout Europe could read it and, as they moved to new countries, the language of music travelled with them. Consequently, most musicians (especially classically trained ones) throughout the world can read music notation, making it possible for a piece written 300 years ago to be interpreted by a living performer today.

**OPPOSITE** Being able to read music will put the great musical works within your grasp. Unlike the handwritten score here, though, most are printed and are much easier to read.

volti

# RHYTHM

## The value of notes

The notes on the music stave take the form of blank and solid black circles, often with a stem. One uncoloured circle constitutes one whole note (or semibreve). The names in brackets in this section indicate older note names, which are still used in some places.

A half note (or minim) is a blank circle with a stem. Quarter notes (or crotchets) look like half notes, but the circles are black. An eighth note (or quaver) looks like a quarter note but has a flag or tail attached to the end of the stem.

A sixteenth note (or semiquaver) has two flags on its stem. A thirty-second note (or demisemiquaver) has three, and a sixty-fourth note (a hemidemisemiquaver!) has four flags on its stem. Simple, isn't it?

### NOTE VALUES

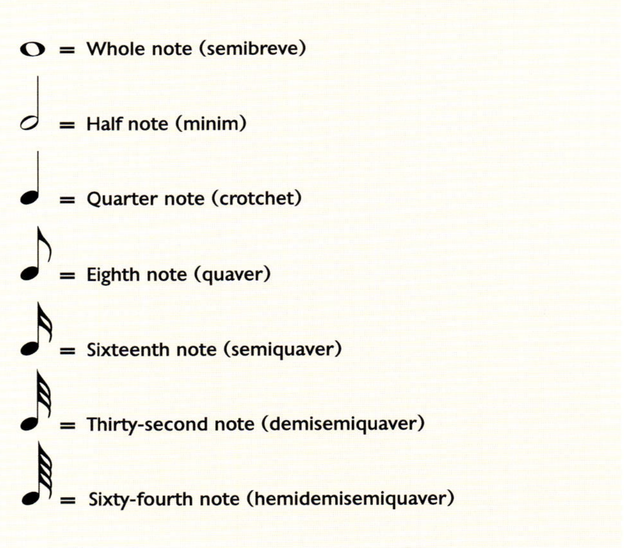


### TIME

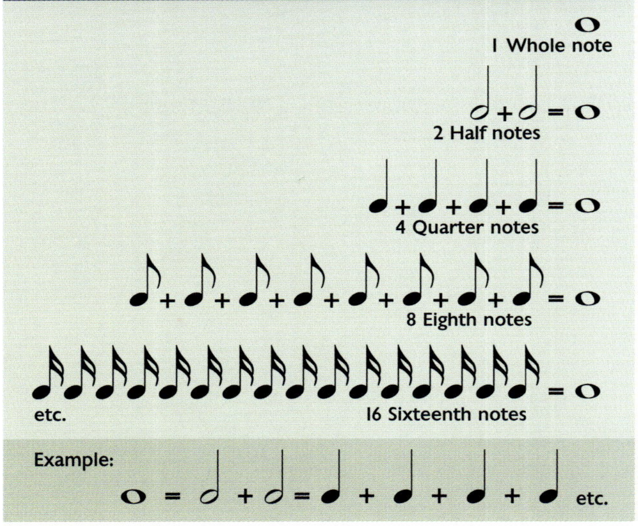


## Time

Music is measured in time. So one half note sounds just as long as two quarter notes and only half the length of one whole note. This does not mean, however, that a quarter note in a slow piece will sound shorter than a half note in a fast piece, because all notes are relative to one another when subjected to tempo (see p26).

This basic mathematics is the foundation of all time in music. In the accompanying graphic (left), the notes on the left add up to form one whole note on the right. Adding two half notes together, for example, gives you a whole note.

The various note values have a relationship in the form of a ratio. A half note's relationship to a whole note forms the ratio 2:1; a quarter note's ratio to a whole note will be 4:1, etc.

## The bar

This is not a place where you have a few drinks, but the space between two vertical bar lines. The bar line runs from the top to the bottom of a stave (those five horizontal lines mentioned in the introduction to this chapter).

Bars divide a piece of music into equal sections. Each bar is given a number (usually starting with one), which is the musician's means of finding a certain place in a piece of music.

Two bar lines of equal thickness next to one another constitute a double bar line, used to divide a piece of music into bigger sections. The final bar line has a thick second line and usually occurs at the end of a piece.

Two dots, one above the other, indicate a repeat, which tells the player to repeat the preceding section.

### THE BAR

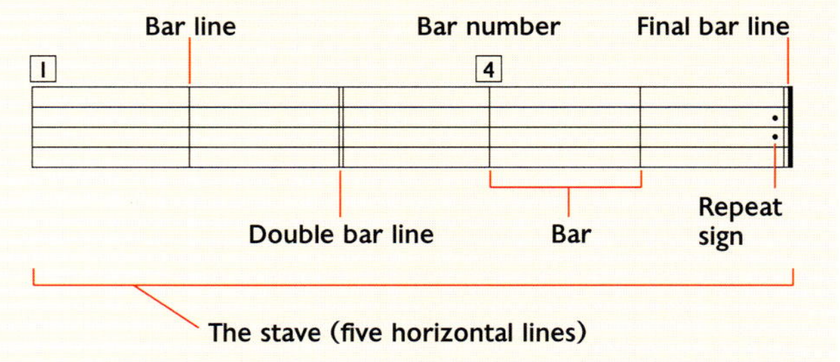


If entire sections of music are repeated, a repeat sign is used to indicate that the preceding section should be played again, rather than duplicating that section.

## Time signature

Most pieces of music have a time signature indicated at the beginning of the piece, written in the form of a fraction, and dividing each bar into equal beats. The top number (usually between 2 and 12) gives the number of beats per bar. The bottom number (any multiple of 2) gives the value of the beat: 2 signifies a half note per beat; 4, a quarter note per beat; 8, an eighth note, and so on. And it is possible for a time signature to change in the middle of a piece. But there are some time signatures which do not conform to this standard. Two of these are **C** and **₵**, which are another way of writing 4/4 and 2/2 respectively. They derive from an obsolete way of indicating time prior to the 17th century, but these specific signs have remained in use.

## Counting the beats

For a novice, it is important to count out loud the beats of a bar while you play and practise. Counting makes you aware of the timing of notes, and it also helps to make sure that all beats are equal in length.

In the illustrative examples, the main beats are indicated by a number above the note that takes the main beat, and subdivisions of the beat are marked with a + sign (spoken as 'and', not 'plus'). Therefore, in the first example below (a), a single bar would be counted as follows: 'One and two and three and'. As you progress, you should be able to read the rhythm of notes without tapping or verbalizing the beat. However, always remain conscious of the fact that there is a constant beat. A metronome (see p90) will help to keep you aware of the beat while you practise, but it is essential to be able to keep a steady beat on your own.

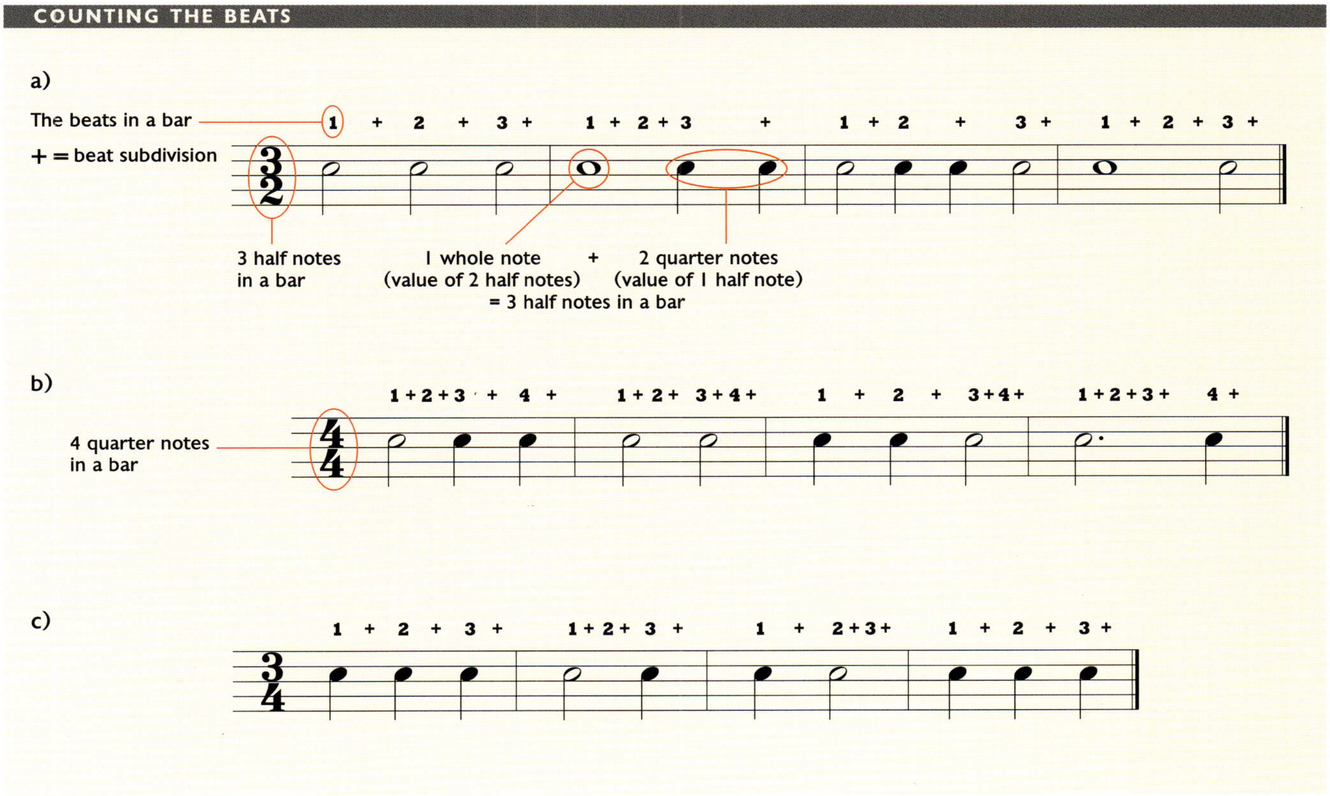

## Rests

Just as there are notes to indicate when a pitch is sounded, there are also rests to denote when there is silence. Each note has a rest which corresponds to it in value.

A whole note rest looks like a small, black rectangle 'hanging' from a line. A half note rest looks the same, but in contrast it 'sits' on a line.

A quarter note rest looks like a squiggle, whereas the 'flagged' notes all have rest signs which look like a '7', with the number of horizontal strokes corresponding with the number of flags on the note.

There is one exception: when a whole bar remains silent a whole note rest is used, no matter what the time signature. Music, like most of the performing arts, needs to breathe and composers use rest signs to achieve this.

RESTS

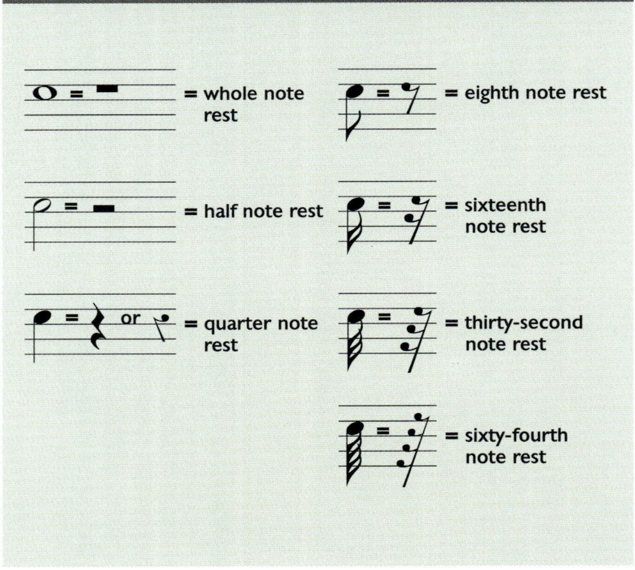


DOTTED NOTES

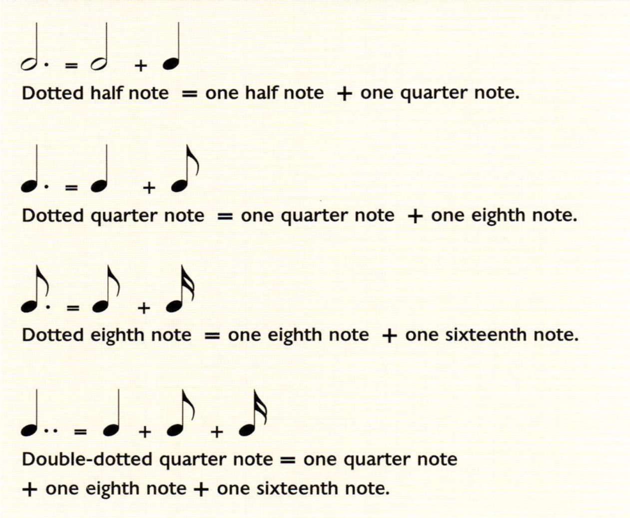


## Dots

A dot on the right of a note lengthens the note by half its value. So, a dotted half note is equal in length to one half note plus one quarter note (or three quarter notes), a dotted quarter note is equal to one quarter note and one eighth note, and a dotted eighth note is equal to one eighth note and one sixteenth note. This rule applies to rests as well.

If a second dot appears on the right of the first dot, it further lengthens the note value by half the value of the previous dot. Thus, a double-dotted half note sounds the composite length of a half note plus a quarter note plus an eighth note (or seven eighth notes).

In music from the 17th and 18th centuries, some dotted notes are played as double-dotted notes, which increases the vitality of the slower music.

## Accents

In a piece of music with a regular beat, some beats are more important than others. In a piece with two beats to a bar (like a march), the first beat is more important than the second beat. In a piece with three beats to a bar (like a waltz), the first beat is more important than the second or third. In a piece with four beats to a bar, the first beat is the most important, the third beat the second most important and the second and fourth beats the least important.

The sign used in music to indicate that a note is further emphasized is called the accent (>). There are many different kinds of accents, but they most often take the form of an arrowhead or triangular shape written above the note they apply to. If an accent falls on a usually unaccented beat, it is referred to as syncopation (see Glossary).

ACCENTS

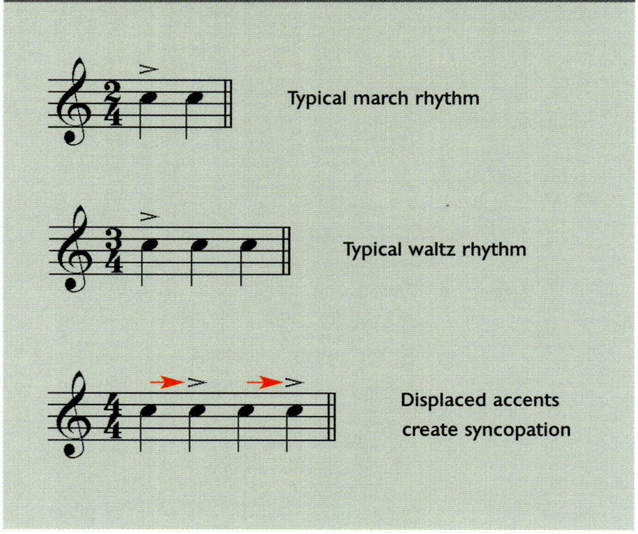

## Groups

Notes are grouped in a certain way within the bar, depending on the time signature. Time signatures with a 2, 3 or 4 as the top value are called simple times because there are only as many groups of notes as there are beats. Time signatures with a 6, 9 or 12 as the top value are called compound times because there are three beats to a group. Following the example, you will see that if there are three beats to a bar (in a simple time signature), the notes will be grouped into three groups. This obviously applies only to notes which are equal to or smaller in value than the value of a beat. Notice how a beam links the notes together. Only notes with flags (tails) are beamed together, with the number of beams corresponding to the number of flags. This looks neater than writing each flagged note separately.

## The tie

Sometimes a composer wants the same note to be played over a bar line or have a note length which does not 'fit' properly in the normal grouping system within a bar. This is achieved by writing two notes, which make up the composite length of the note he wishes to hear, so that they 'tie' together using a curved line. This line extends from one notehead to the other, either over the bar line or between two notes within the same bar. A tie is used only between two notes of the same pitch, otherwise it's a slur (see p36).

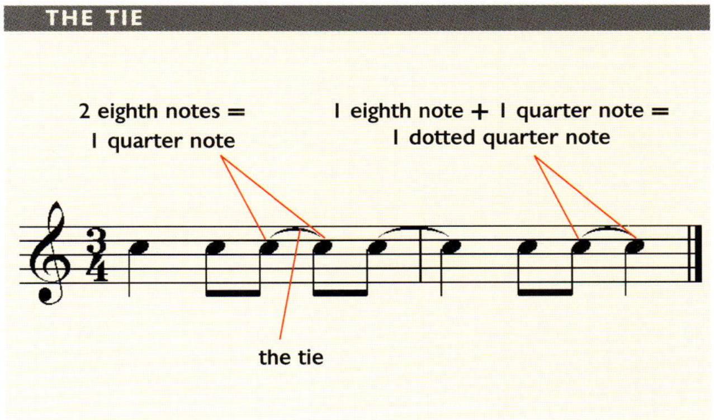


## Rhythm exercise

Congratulations! You are now well on your way to reading music. The exercise below should help you read musical rhythm. It can be either clapped or sung on any vowel to your liking. Count the beats written above the notes. Make sure your beats are of equal length. Do not start practising too fast. Start slowly and speed up later.

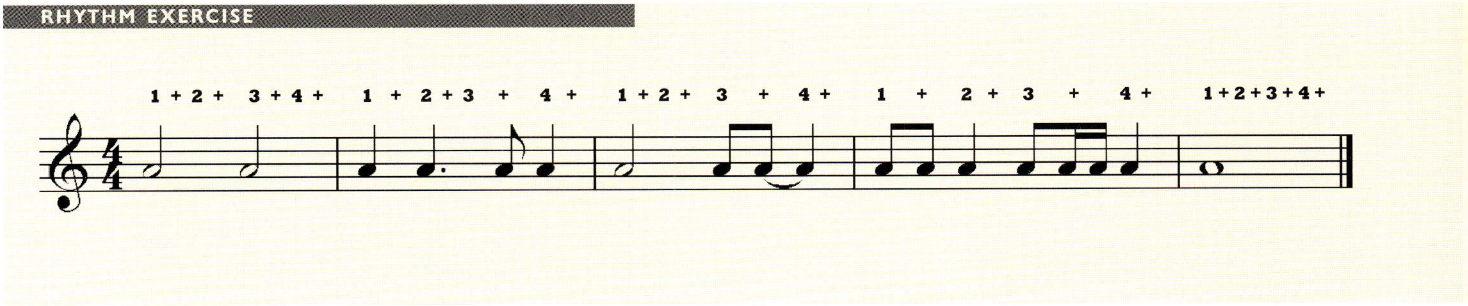

# PITCH

## Positions on the fingerboard

All aspects of pitch on the violin have to do with the fingerboard, the position of the fingers of your left hand, and what string you are on. This applies whether you are right- or left-handed, since there is only one way of holding the violin. When you want to produce a certain note, you have to 'stop' one of the four strings. Stopping a string means pressing down on the string at a specific point, thereby reducing its vibrating length and producing the correct note.

What makes the violin so difficult (especially in the beginning) is that you have to stop the string on exactly the right spot, otherwise your note will be out of tune (even if the strings are in tune – see p31). On a guitar, you have frets and you can (theoretically) stop the string anywhere between two frets to produce the correct note. This is why the guitar is, in many respects, easier to learn and play than the violin.

To aid you in negotiating the fingerboard on the violin, most teachers and books refer to the various 'positions' on the fingerboard. These are characterized as either low positions (1–4) or high positions (5–8). The lower the number of the position, the closer it is to the nut, and the higher the position, the closer it is to the bridge. Most beginners are restricted to the low positions on the fingerboard since the high positions can be very tricky to master. Most of the pieces and exercises in this book are in first position.

**ABOVE LEFT** The closer your fingers are to the bridge, the higher the notes you will produce.
**ABOVE RIGHT** The further your fingers move away from the bridge, towards the nut, the lower the notes will sound.

## Finger frames

Each position on the fingerboard has a number of 'finger frames'. This refers to the combination of distances between the four fingers of the left hand used to stop notes. In violin fingering, the number 1 (see below) always refers to the index finger and 4 to the little finger. The rest is obvious. It is especially important to pay attention to this next section if you want to make head or tail of the rest of this book.

The finger frames in the image below are all in first position. The horizontal line at the top represents the nut. The vertical line represents the string. A blank circle represents a space the width of a finger between the fingers (or one semitone – see next page). A solid black circle represents a finger (stopping the string) and the numbers to the left of each solid circle refer to the corresponding finger.

The first finger frame is the standard, with the space of a semitone between 1st and 2nd finger and between 3rd and 4th finger. The rest of the finger frames are based on the first one. If a minus (-) precedes the finger number, the finger has shifted one space (semitone) back (closer to the nut). If a plus (+) precedes the finger number, the finger has shifted one space (semitone) forward (closer to the bridge).

**FINGER FRAMES**

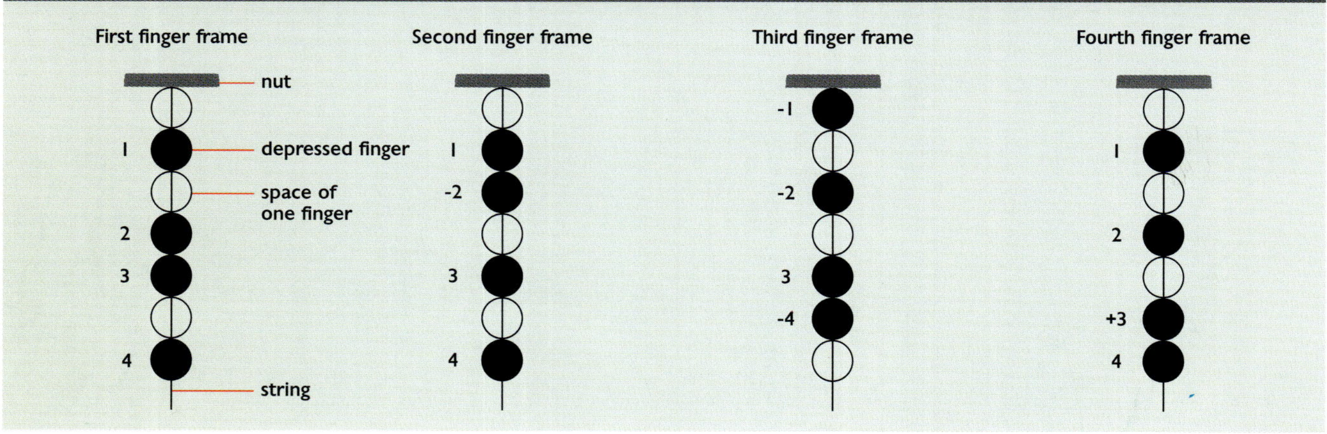

## The stave

The biggest difficulty when reading music is to translate a note on the stave into an action on the fingerboard which will result in the correct note. Before you get to that stage, however, I want to discuss the stave and the difference between the written notes and the physical action that produces them. The stave consists of five horizontal lines. A note is either on a line or in the space between two lines. The pitch of a note depends on its position on the stave. The higher the note is on the stave, the higher it will sound. If notes go higher or lower than the stave allows, a ledger line is used. This has the same function as the rest of the lines, but is used only for a specific note. Bear in mind that the stave does not represent the strings of the violin.

THE STAVE

## The strings

Each string, apart from its designation as 1st, 2nd, 3rd and 4th string, has another name. The name corresponds to the note to which that string is tuned. The 1st string (or the highest-sounding string) is called the E-string and the note is written in the 4th space on the stave. The 2nd string is the A-string, written in the 2nd space. The 3rd string is the D-string (written in the 1st space below the stave) and the 4th string is the low G-string, written in the space below the second ledger line. These names refer to the open or 'unstopped' strings.

The open strings of a violin are tuned in fifths. This means that they are five notes apart when written, and sound the interval of a fifth apart. An interval refers to the distance between notes. It is vital that you memorize the sound of a fifth (the first notes of *Twinkle Twinkle Little Star*) for tuning purposes (see p31).

THE STRINGS

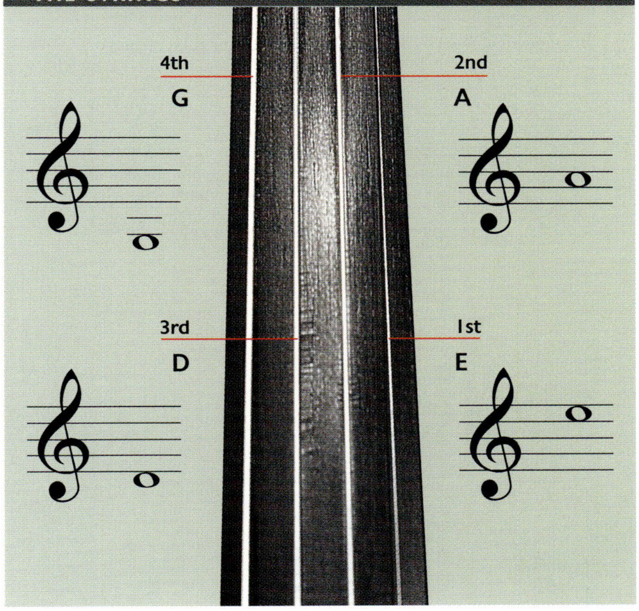


## Tones and semitones

Tones and semitones form an important part of intervals and you need to understand what they are before moving on to the next section. Think back to the finger frames (previous page). The distance of one semitone separates all the circles. A semitone is the smallest distance between two notes. As you may have guessed, two semitones form a tone. So, in the first finger frame, the 1st and 2nd fingers are a tone apart whereas the 2nd and 3rd fingers are a semitone apart. Be aware that this has nothing to do with rhythm, but with the difference in pitch between two notes.

TONES AND SEMITONES

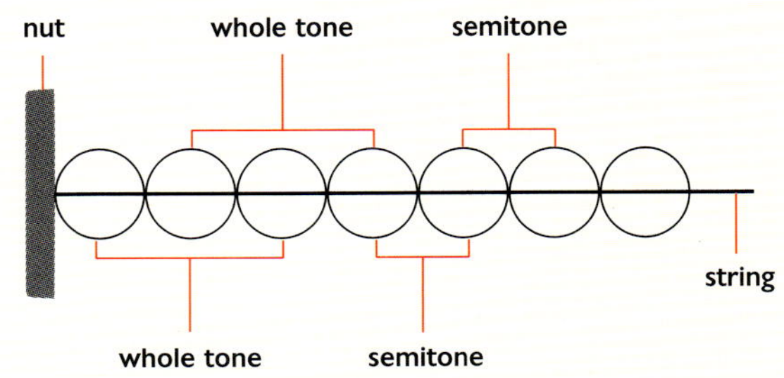

## Note names

Notes in music take their names from the first seven letters of the alphabet. The note A is written in the second space on the stave. The note on the line above it (the third line) is B. The note in the next space (the third space) is C, and so forth. When you get to the G in the space just above the stave, the next note, on the first ledger line above the stave, is A again. This A is said to be an octave above the previous A because it is eight notes above it (from the Latin 'octo' meaning eight). This naming system works in both directions. Therefore, the note on the line below the first A is G. The note in the first space below G is F, and so on.

The notes are divided into those above middle C (the C in the middle of the piano keyboard) and those below it. Clef signs are used to specify the register of notes. The treble clef 𝄞 – or G clef, because it starts on the second line, which is G – generally indicates notes above middle C, whereas the bass clef 𝄢 is used for notes below middle C. Since most of the violin's notes are above middle C, violin music is written exclusively in the treble clef.

## Accidentals

There are 12 semitones in an octave (you will have to take my word for it) but only seven letters (A to G) to name them. Therefore, signs were developed to either raise or lower a note by a semitone. These signs are called accidentals.

The sharp sign [♯], written before a note, is used to raise a note by a semitone. A flat sign [♭], written before a note, is used to lower a note by a semitone.

In the illustration below, all the possible semitones in one octave in first position have been indicated according to string. Notice that the last semitone on each string is the same as the open note of the next string.

**NOTE NAMES**

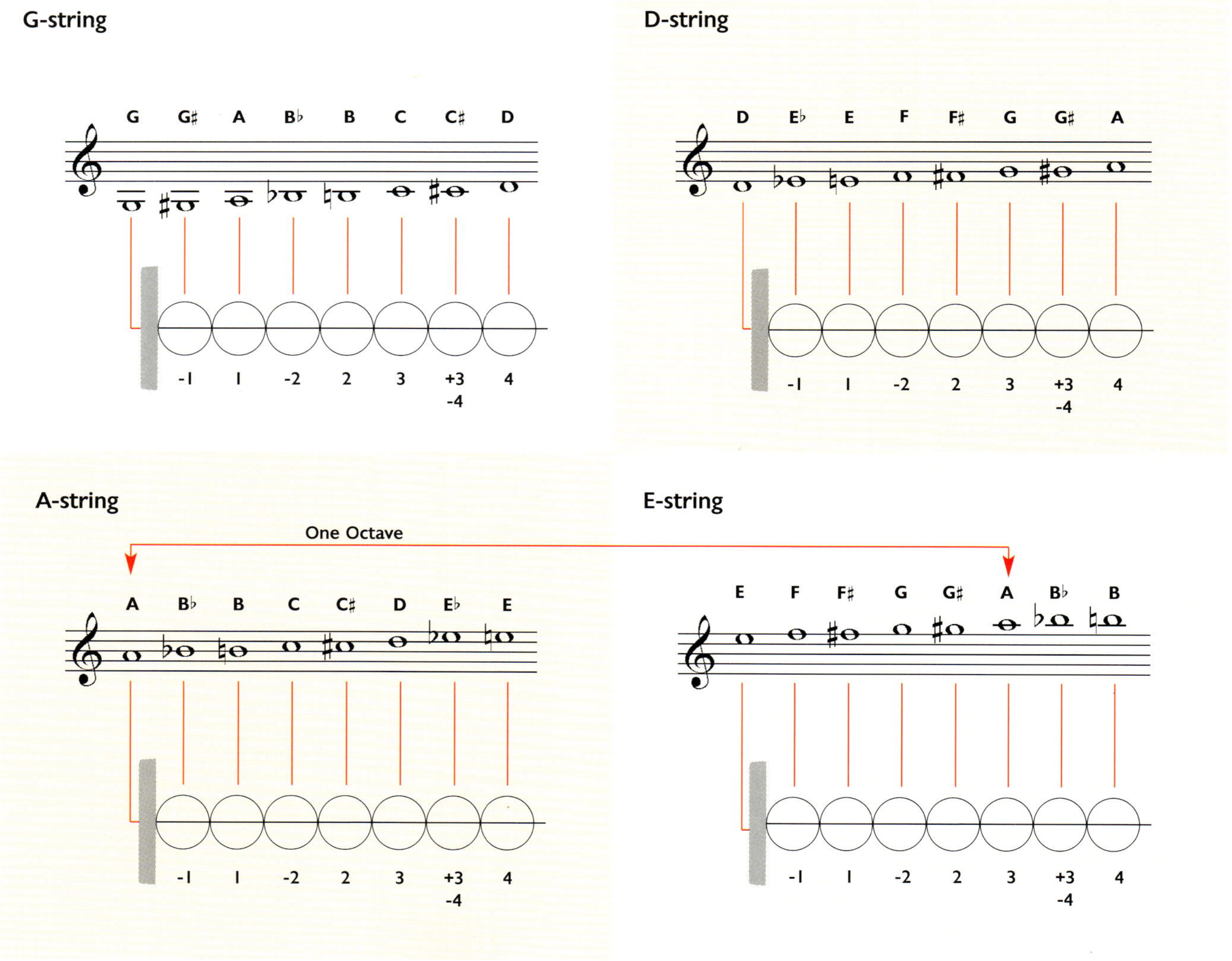

## Double names

Using the third note (circle) on the G-string as an example, you can see that the note can be written either as an A which has been sharpened, or as a B which has been flattened. Therefore, all these notes can have two names (theoretically) even though they sound the same.

The only exceptions are the notes B and C and E and F, which are already a semitone apart. They also have two names. B can also be written as a flattened C and C can also be written as a sharpened B. The same applies to E and F. This may seem a bit complicated at first, but do try to understand it, because once you do there will be no more mysteries concerning pitch in written music.

DOUBLE NAMES

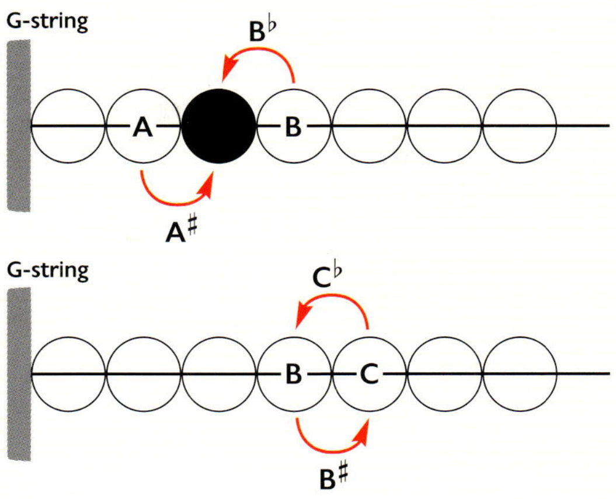


## Key signature

A key signature is a collection of sharps or flats at the beginning of a piece of music, denoting that all subsequent notes on that pitch are altered. So, if an F-sharp appears at the beginning of the piece as a key signature, all Fs in the piece are sharpened, unless they are altered by a natural sign [♮].

All seven of the 'normal' notes are said to be in their 'natural' state, but the natural sign is written before a note to distinguish it from a previous inflection (sharp or flat). This natural sign alters subsequent notes only in the same bar, the bar line once again enforcing the key signature.

There is an order in which sharps and flats are introduced into a key signature. The first sharp is always F-sharp. The next is C-sharp. So, if a piece has a key signature of one sharp it is always F-sharp. If it has two sharps they are always F-sharp and C-sharp. The order in which sharps appear is F, C, G, D, A, E and B. Flats are introduced into a key signature exactly the other way around (B, E, A, D, G, C and F).

KEY SIGNATURE

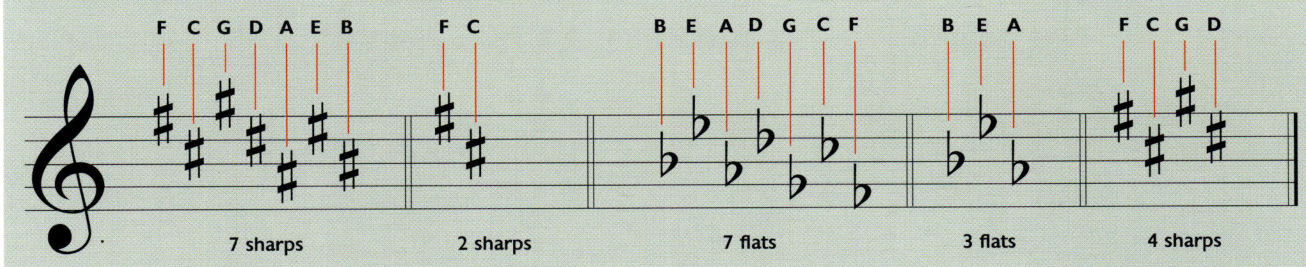


## Exercises

This is as tough as it gets. If you can manage to name the notes in the following exercises, you should have few problems recognizing written pitch. They are written exercises – do not attempt them on the violin just yet. The rhythm of all the notes in each exercise is equal.

EXERCISES

## Tempo

Apart from rhythm and pitch, there are various signs and symbols in written music. It takes years to get to know them all, because you can only really understand something if it occurs in a piece you are playing rather than in a long list of terms you have learned by heart. One set of terms falls under the general heading of tempo indications. These are words usually written in the top left-hand corner of a piece of music. They describe how fast or slow or the general character in which the piece should be played. A piece with many sections might have multiple tempo indications, but they are always written above the stave. (For a list of more words and their explanation, consult the Glossary at the end of the book.)

**TEMPO**

Adagio – Slowly and at leisure
Andante – Moderately slow and at a walking pace
Allegro – Fast and in a lively manner
Presto – Very fast
♩ = 100 – means 100 quarter notes per minute
♩ = c.100 – means approximately 100 quarter notes per minute
Accelerando – Accel. – becoming gradually faster
Ritardando – Rit. – becoming gradually slower
Grave – slow and solemn

## Dynamics

There are also many words, abbreviations and symbols which refer to the dynamic character of a piece of music (how loud or soft and when it changes from one to the other). These words or abbreviations indicate the dynamics or volume of an entire piece or certain groups of notes. They are usually written below the stave.

**DYNAMICS**

| | | |
|---|---|---|
| Fortissimo | ***ff*** | very loud |
| Forte | ***f*** | loud |
| Mezzo forte | ***mf*** | half (moderately) loud |
| Mezzo piano | ***mp*** | half (moderately) soft |
| Piano | ***p*** | soft |
| Pianissimo | ***pp*** | very soft |
| Crescendo | < | getting gradually louder |
| Decrescendo | > | getting gradually softer |

**BELOW** The American composer George Gershwin (1898–1937) composing at the piano.

Rhythm and pitch are equal partners in music and the one is definitely useless without the other. But the most difficult thing to do when reading music is to concentrate on both. Luckily, you can practise this skill. Here are some tips on how to read and practise reading effectively.

- Read as much music as possible. Just as your reading speed increases if you read a lot of books, so it is the same with reading music.
- Read music as often as possible until it becomes second nature. Rather than reading music for an hour each week, read music for 10 minutes each day.
- Read ahead. Try to keep your eyes one bar ahead of your hands. This may sound impossible, especially to a beginner, but it does happen eventually.
- Concentrate on rhythm first because you can read it faster than pitch. When reading ahead, assess the rhythm of the entire bar instantaneously (it is easier than you think). This leaves you free to concentrate on pitch.

Obviously this skill develops only over time. Do not feel disheartened if you do not achieve the results immediately. It takes a lot of time and patience to learn how to read music, especially if you are struggling to master a new instrument. You are conditioning your brain to translate symbols into movements, which then turn into sounds. Of course it is going to take time and energy – just like other worthwhile things in life. However, do not give up. If you practise sight-reading regularly, it is impossible for you not to succeed. Remember also that once you have superior sight-reading capabilities, the world of music is your oyster.

**ABOVE** The Russian violinist Viktoria Mullova (b.1959) rehearses with the BBC Philharmonic Orchestra, July 2000.

chapter three

# PRACTISE BEFORE PLAYING

THERE ARE MANY WAYS TO PLAY THE VIOLIN. One teacher will expect you to hold the bow in a certain way while another might throw you out of his or her class for perpetrating such blasphemy. So do not be alarmed if you pick up another book and find a different set of teachings. The most important thing is that you play the violin in the way that gives you the greatest pleasure.

It is tempting for beginners to disregard the normal conventions in the hope that they will pick things up as they go along. Just remember that the longer you practise bad habits, the more difficult it is going to be to rectify them later. Therefore, if you are serious in your wish to play the violin, it is worth taking the trouble to learn the 'correct' way from the beginning. I recommend that you find a good teacher as soon as possible (see p92), for the violin is not really an instrument which can be self-taught (although it has been done).

Over the years your technique (a grand word for the way in which you play) and your physical ability will be moulded, modified and shaped by various teachers until you reach the point where you have developed your own true style. This is what sets the great artists apart from musicians who follow a set of teachings rigidly – the ability to adapt.

This chapter is concerned with developing your technique and the actual mechanics of playing the violin. To this end, I have included various technical exercises to help you. You will also be taught (as far as it is possible from a book) to hold the violin and its bow correctly and how to produce the various notes on the instrument.

Many things you learn here will be tested on your own or a hired instrument. Do not be alarmed by the discomfort of many of the positions, particularly if you are an adult. The adult body is not as flexible as that of a child and it may take a while for your limbs and muscles to become used to the mechanical actions of violin playing. Do not fret. It does become easier.

**OPPOSITE** Although many beginners are daunted by the thought of repetitive practice, it is really the only way to progress beyond the basics of learning to play music.

## Preparing yourself

Your body is your tool for making music and therefore is just as important as the instrument. So make sure you are in good condition if you are serious about wanting to play music. Eating healthy food, getting adequate sleep and enough exercise and cultivating a general sense of wellbeing are all essential in playing an instrument well.

It is also important to prepare yourself mentally before you even pick up the violin, be it to practise or to perform. Start by closing your eyes and taking long, steadying breaths. Then proceed to warm up the various joints and muscles you are going to be using. This includes stretching the muscles in your arms, shoulders, neck, back, wrists and fingers.

Once you feel loose and relaxed and in the right state of mind, open the case and pick up your violin.

## Preparing the violin

Just like your body, the violin has to be prepared before you start playing. Begin by carefully taking the violin out of its case and rubbing the body and strings lightly with a soft, dry cloth to get rid of any dust or rosin.

Now attach the shoulder rest and adjust it to the correct position and height (see p32–33). Be sure to keep the violin at the correct angle from the start.

Gently pick up the bow and turn the adjuster until the ribbon of the bow is tight enough. Be careful not to make it too tight. Test the bow by 'bouncing' it lightly on an outstretched finger (while holding onto the frog) so that the finger hits the middle of the ribbon. The ribbon is sufficiently taut if it gives way, but without your finger touching the wooden part of the bow.

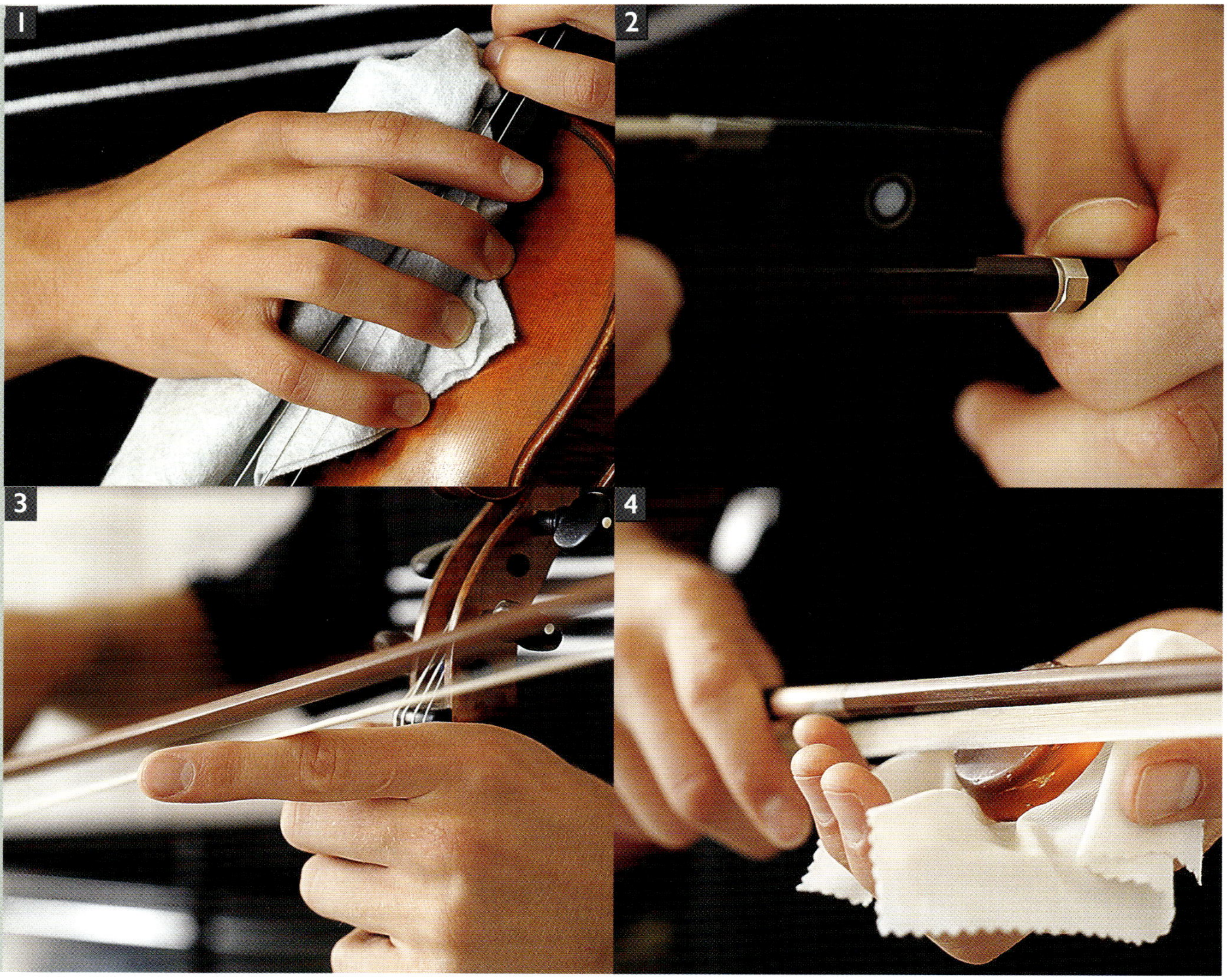


**CLOCKWISE FROM TOP LEFT** Some of the preparatory steps you need to take before you start playing include: (1) wiping the instrument gently with a soft cloth to remove any dust; (2) tightening the ribbon with the adjuster; (3) checking its tautness by bouncing it against your finger; and (4) dusting the ribbon lightly with some rosin.

Pull the ribbon over a piece of rosin repeatedly until it is lightly but sufficiently 'dusted'. Now you are ready to begin playing – if your violin is in tune.

## Tuning the violin

There are many ways to tune a violin, but the best for a beginner is to get the correct pitch for each string from a tuning fork, pitch pipe or keyboard. Also ask your teacher to teach you the best way to tune your instrument. Bear in mind that pitch pipes distort the note if you blow too hard and they go out of tune as they get older.

Start by tuning the A-string. Play the correct note on the tuning fork or whatever instrument you are using for the pitch and listen to the sound. Play the note again and memorize the sound. Now play the open string. If the sound is too high, loosen the string, and if it is too low, tighten it.

If the difference between the open string and the tuning instrument is very noticeable, you will have to use the tuning pegs. Always begin by loosening the string and then 'tuning it up'. When you have the correct pitch you must apply pressure to the tuning peg to force it deeper into its hole in the pegbox so that it does not slip. When playing the violin together with another instrument, the two different sounds can make it hard to hear whether you have the correct note, so it would be best to memorize the reference pitch before you tune the violin.

If the difference between the open string and the tuning instrument is minimal, you can adjust the note with the fine tuners, located on the tailpiece. The note will be in tune if you play the open string while a partner sounds the tuning instrument and you cannot hear any 'waviness' in the sound. The more waves, the more out of tune you are.

Now repeat the procedure with the D-string. If you have only the A as a reference note, bow or pluck the D-string and then the A-string. If you know the sound of a fifth (which you will before long), play the two strings simultaneously and adjust the one that is out of tune. If you do not know what a fifth sounds like, ask someone, like a teacher, to tune your violin for you and make sure you imprint the sound of the four strings into your memory.

Now repeat the entire procedure with the G-string, playing the G- and D-strings together to hear the fifth.

Lastly, play the E-string and tune it to the A-string by playing them together to get the fifth.

Do not worry if this all sounds a bit complicated. By the third week you will be doing this without thinking. If you have ever heard an orchestra 'tuning up' before a symphony concert you will realise that you have been doing just that.

**TOP** If there is a large difference in pitch, start by tuning the string from the tuning pegs.
**ABOVE** The fine tuners can be used to make minimal adjustments to the pitch.

## Body posture and holding the violin

This is the one aspect of violin playing that can be the most varied. All bodies are different so what works for one person may not work for another. A good general rule to apply is that you must feel free and comfortable when playing, and develop a good centre of gravity. You can play the violin while standing or sitting. Accustom yourself to both variations, since both are used in the world of violin playing.

When sitting, sit up straight. Imagine a line running from your head to the place where you come in contact with the chair. Strive to keep this line straight, but not rigid or unbending. Do not lean against the back of the chair but sit forward with one leg further out than the other. This gives you better balance than symmetrical legs do.

When standing, spread your weight over both legs. Keep your feet apart and in line with your shoulders. For better balance I recommend that you place the left foot slightly in front of the right. Do not move it too far forward or you may end up putting most of your weight on this foot, which will inhibit the movement of your upper body. However, if you have to put more weight on a specific foot, make it the left foot, since you need to keep the bowing half of your body (the right) as free as possible.

Your upper body is the more active part of you when it comes to violin playing. But in fact you are playing with your entire body, not just your arms, so become body conscious and really be aware what each bit of you is doing. Your chest should be open and your shoulders pulled slightly backwards. You are presenting yourself to an audience and no one likes to look at a person with poor posture.

Too much movement will detract from the music since it forces you to constantly readjust your grip on the bow. Too little movement, on the other hand, will give you a wooden appearance and may lead to general stiffness.

**ABOVE AND LEFT** Whether you are standing or sitting down, the correct posture and method of holding the violin are essential if you are to play comfortably and well.

The violin rests on your left collarbone (1). Many modern instruments come with a shoulder rest and a chin rest. Place the shoulder rest on your shoulder and hold the violin in your left hand at about 40 degrees to the outside of your body (2).

Place your chin on the chin rest but not squarely in the hollow, otherwise you will have to bend your neck too much. Your chin should rest on the side of the chin rest, more towards the middle of the violin. Make sure that your chin does not touch the tailpiece. You should be able to hold the violin in place without supporting it with the left hand.

Keep the scroll at the appropriate height, as in the illustration (2, above). A good rule is to have the scroll at a slightly higher position, since your body will then support most of the weight of the violin. Otherwise, it should be parallel to the floor

## The left arm and hand

Imagine the left arm supported from the shoulder. You can visualize the arm 'hanging' from the fingerboard, but support is necessary. The 'hanging' also allows you to utilize the effect of gravity of your arm when stopping the strings.

Your elbow should hang naturally beneath the instrument. The length of your fingers will determine this. The shorter your fingers, the more to the right your elbow must move. Do not keep the position of the elbow rigid, since your arm will have to move flexibly around on the fingerboard.

Your wrist, in general, should not allow any sideways curve in the hand and should align with the forearm (3). In some positions, this will obviously not be possible, but it is a good general rule. Your wrist should never 'collapse' inwards because this reduces its flexibility and you will have trouble shifting your hand position later.

The hand should remain in light contact with both sides of the fingerboard (try to imagine that you are caressing the fingerboard). The index finger will remain in contact with the fingerboard until the fourth position. Too much pressure exerted by the index finger will cause the neck to move too far to the left. Also make sure you do not angle the hand too far backwards, as this makes stopping with the fourth finger very difficult.

Your fingers must fall vertically (with the fleshy part of the fingertip) onto the string (4). When you have stopped the string, the fingers will not be completely vertical, but when in their usual place (the first finger frame – refer to p22), they should form a 'square' shape.

As your fingers move around (finger frames 2–4) the angle of the various fingers will become more slanted. Less fleshy fingertips will have to slant slightly backwards.

**TOP** (1) The adjustable shoulder rest will help you find the correct and most comfortable height for the violin.
(2) Hold the violin at a 40° angle to the horizontal line of your shoulders.
(3) The wrist holding the neck of the violin must stay in line with the arm and never 'collapse' inwards.
(4) When stopping a string, stop it from above but keep your hand relaxed as you do so.

The thumb acts as a counter to the pressure exerted by the stopping fingers and should not protrude too high above the fingerboard. A rule of thumb (ha ha) is: the longer the thumb, the further it will protrude. Also try not to press too hard with the thumb against the fingerboard – you might turn your hand into an unmoving, uncomfortable clamp.

A general rule for the entire left arm, elbow, hand and fingers is this: you must be relaxed and free in your movements so that your fingers can move around on the fingerboard when they have to.

## The right arm and hand

The bow is an extension of the arm and the two should function as one. To this end, a flow and ease of movement is essential. The whole bowing mechanism functions like a spring and it is this 'springiness' that has to be taken into account when bowing notes on the violin.

The bow hold you are learning here is generally referred to as the basic or neutral hold, or grip. It gives a full, round sound but, even so, you will have to change and modify your hold constantly to fit the style and intensity of the music you are playing. This takes many years, so be content with mastering the basic hold before moving on to others.

The basic hold utilizes the natural hand position. Start by relaxing your hand and forming a circle with your thumb and index finger. Holding the bow with the left hand (point in the air with the ribbon facing you), move your right hand over the bow at the frog. The inside of the thumb should be in contact with the underside of the lapping, near the cutout of the frog. The thumb, which acts as a platform for the bow, should not protrude on the other side of the bow (see above).

Now rest the index finger on the stick (the wooden part of the bow), keeping the initial circle with the thumb. The middle finger should rest (at the second joint) on the metal-wound part of the lower bow, the rest of the finger curving slightly over the stick.

The middle and ring fingers will be closer together. Bend them over the stick. The tip of your ring finger should be in contact with the side of the frog (see above left), while the middle finger should be in line with the thumb.

The little finger rests on the top of the stick (close to the adjuster) and supplies a counter-pressure against the thumb. It should be possible for you to hold the bow using only thumb and little finger.

If you ever feel your bowing hand tensing up, becoming stiff or unbending, you can free it by relaxing each finger's grip on the bow (one at a time) and tapping the finger gently against the bow. You can also 're-activate' the springiness of your hand by scrunching up the fingers, thereby pulling the bow closer to your palm, and then 'releasing' them again.

**TOP LEFT** Notice the placement of the index, middle, ring and little fingers for the basic hold.

**TOP RIGHT** The placing of the thumb is very important in providing counter-pressure for the little finger.

## Bowing

The art of bowing is a subtle science and requires a whole book to explain it adequately. But I will discuss the basic bowing technique, which should be enough to get you going.

Start by placing the bottom of the bow (near the frog) on the A-string in the middle of the gap between the bridge and the fingerboard. The bow should form a 90-degree angle with the string. Also try to make the entire ribbon come into contact with the string.

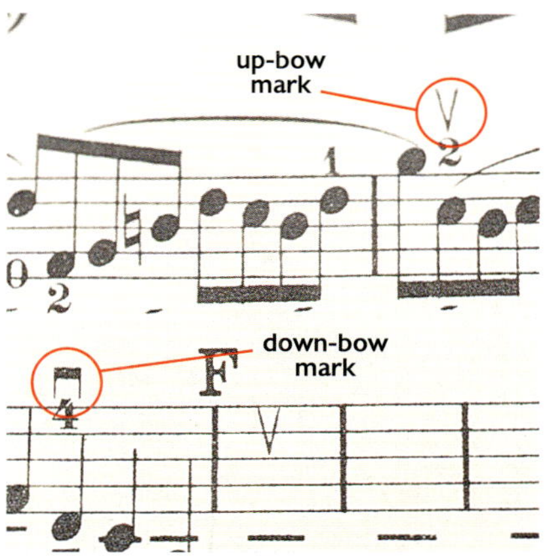


Now bow the string with the entire length of the bow (all the way to the point). Make certain the angle between the bow and string remains at 90 degrees and the entire ribbon remains in contact with the string. Bow from the elbow, so that only the elbow-joint bends, allowing your lower arm to do the movement. Using a mirror will help you keep the bow at the right angle and parallel to the bridge.

You will notice that you had to bend your wrist to compensate for the angle between bow and string. This is perfectly correct. The higher (pitch wise) the string, the more you will have to compensate in this way. A good way to practise loosening your wrist is to simulate the bowing action (without the bow) and touch your nose with your wrist. You will only be able to do this if you keep your upper arm stationary and bend your wrist accordingly (otherwise you will punch yourself in the face with your fist).

This bowing action, from the frog in the direction of the point, is called a down-bow (because the action is mostly downward). In printed music for the violin, it is indicated mostly above the stave by a [⊓]. An up-bow takes place by bowing from the point in the direction of the frog. It is indicated by a [V].

The last aspect of simple bowing is that you can play with different parts of the bow. The term 'full bow' means you play with the entire length of the bow. 'Half bow' means the bowing action utilizes only half the bow length. There are no general rules for using one or the other, but as your playing and knowledge progress, it will become obvious where to use which bowing action.

**ABOVE** (1) When bowing throughout the length of the bow, it is important to maintain a 90° angle between the bow and the strings.
(2) Most of the bowing action is done using the lower arm and the wrist.
(3) When bowing near the frog, the wrist has to bend to keep the 90° angle between the bow and the strings.
**TOP** Bowing marks are especially important in orchestral music, to synchronize the bowing movements of a group of players.

## Articulation

Articulation refers to the types of up- and down-bows within a piece of music, as well as the nature of the bowing action itself. There are quite a few, but the most important ones have been included here. You will not get to learn or use many of them until much later, but at least you will know what they are should you encounter them in other books or pieces of music.

***Legato*** – This method of bowing tries to make notes flow smoothly from one to the other, without any breaks or gaps between them. It is indicated by a slur and should not be confused with the tie (see p21). A slur can be written over a group of notes of different pitch and means that all the notes under it must be bowed in the same bow-stroke (either up or down).

***Détaché*** – This is the 'usual' way of bowing separated notes, where the direction of the bowing changes for each note. If the notes are to be played very fast, then you obviously will not be able to use full bows. This type of bowing takes place when there are no slur or other *legato* indications. The composer may specify if you are to play the notes at the point (*a punta d'arco*) or at the frog (*al tallone*).

***Staccato*** – This indication means that the notes should be played with short, separate strokes, almost like *détaché*, but shorter. The notes must have a 'clipped' character. *Staccato* is indicated by a dot above or below the notehead (not to be confused with the dot next to the notehead – see p20).

***Louré*** – This means that a slight separation of notes should occur while the bow is being drawn, and takes place on one bowing (either up or down). It usually refers to a group of notes on the same pitch and is indicated by *tenuto* signs (a short horizontal stripe below the notehead) under a slur.

***Martelé*** – Meaning 'hammered', this is the most violent form of articulation in which each note is played with a fast, well-articulated, heavy, separate stroke. *Martelé* is indicated when a group of consecutive notes has accents (>, Λ) written above them. Do not confuse the second accent with the up-bow sign, which is the other way around.

***Spiccato*** – This articulation usually occurs in fast, light (sometimes soft) passages of music. It involves either a conscious or spontaneous bouncing of the bow on the strings while playing the notes.

**LEGATO**

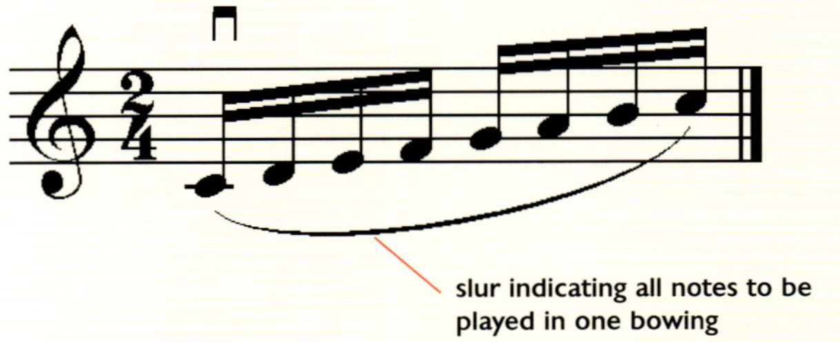


**STACCATO**

**LOURÉ**

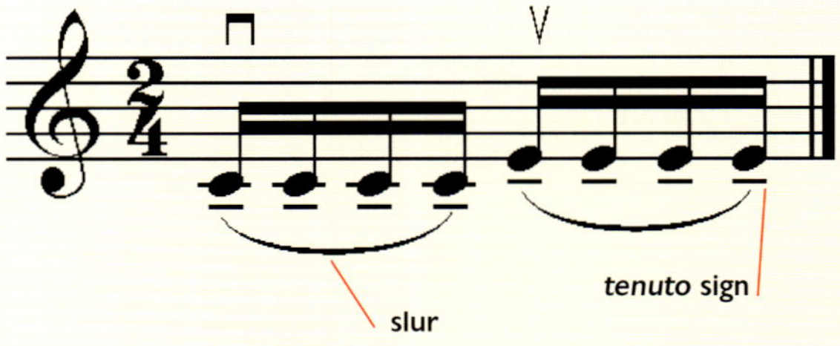


**MARTELÉ**

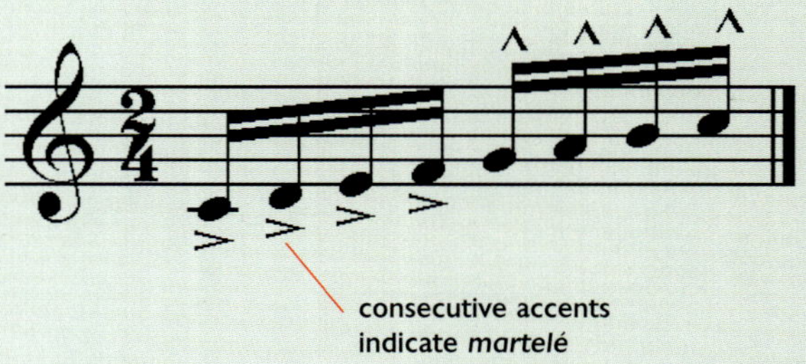


***Jété*** – Meaning 'jumped' or 'thrown', this articulation is affected by 'throwing' the upper third of the bow onto the string, thereby causing it to bounce and result in a succession of between two and six rapid notes.

## Sound effects

The nature of the violin as a string instrument means that a host of sound effects is possible. Once again, you will not encounter many of these until later, but having more knowledge than necessary is always a good thing. Many of these are especially important to know if you are going to play in an orchestra (see p80).

***Vibrato*** – This happens when you rotate the wrist of the left hand or 'vibrate' the fingers, thereby causing an undulation in the note produced. It is especially effective on long notes and gives the sound a warm, soulful quality.

***Trill*** – Indicated by '(tr)' and often also a wavy line written above a note, this means that you have to finger that specific note and a note next to it (of either a semitone or a tone), alternating quickly between the two notes for the entire value of the note specified, keeping the lower finger down.

***Tremolo*** – This sounds very much like a *trill*, but occurs between two notes more than a tone or semitone apart. It can be fingered (on the same string) or bowed (between two adjacent strings). It can also occur on one pitch, thereby causing a rapid repetition of that note. Short slanted lines through the stem of the notes involved indicates a *tremolo*. It can also mean to play the notes as fast as possible.

***Glissando*** – This means you have to literally 'slide' your finger from one note to another on the fingerboard. It is indicated by a slanted line between the two notes.

***Pizzicato*** – When you see this word or its abbreviation (*pizz.*) you stop bowing and pluck all the notes with the index finger of the bowing hand. The effect is cancelled by the word '*arco*', which means you start bowing normally again.

***Sul ponticallo*** – Meaning 'on the bridge' this indicates that you have to bow near (or even on) the bridge. The tone produced has a glassy, metallic, eerie quality.

***Sul tasto*** – This means that you bow near the fingerboard. It produces a soft, delicate, velvety sound.

***Col legno*** – This term literally means 'with the wood' and instructs you to strike the string with the wooden part of the bow. The sound produced is very soft, because of less traction, but it can also be eerie and percussive and is used to great effect en masse.

***Con sordino*** – This means you should play with a mute (see p90). When a composer writes this instruction on the score, he will usually give the player enough time to move the mute onto the bridge, thereby changing the sound dramatically from loud and strident to soft and delicate. The term *senza sordino* cancels the mute.

That, in a nutshell, is it.

**TRILL**

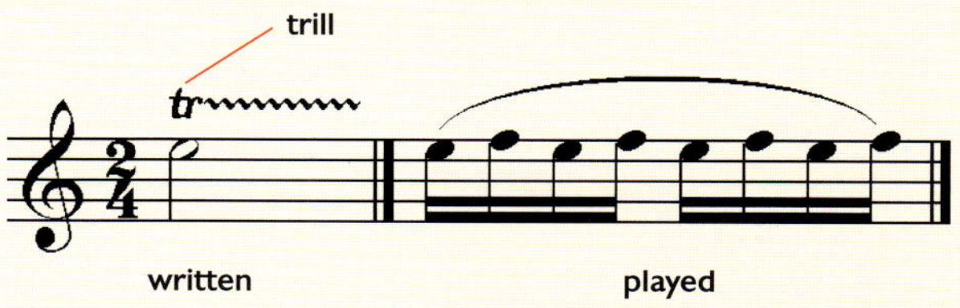


**TREMOLO 1**

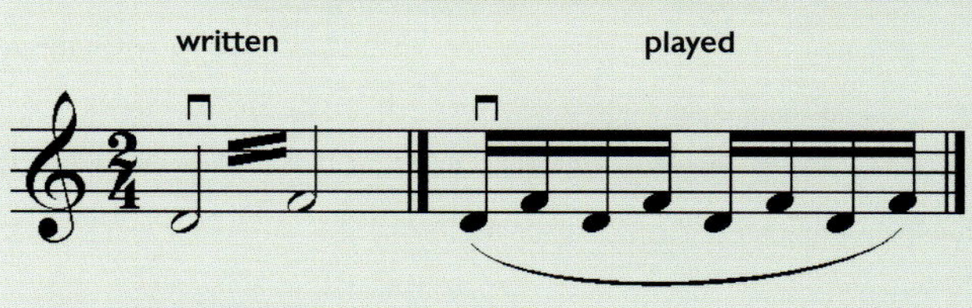


a fingered *tremolo* (on the same string)

**TREMOLO 2**

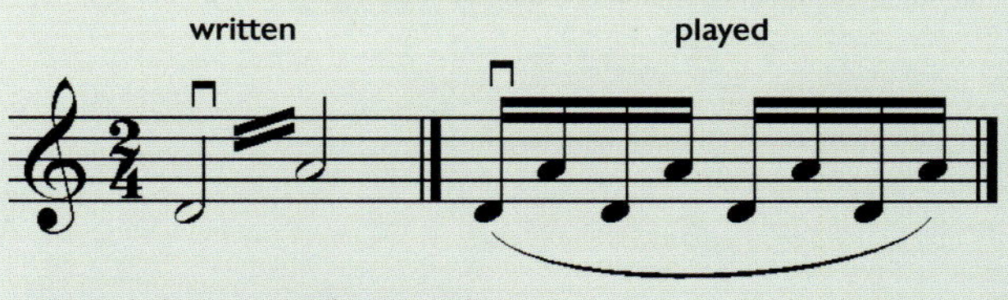


a *tremolo* between adjacent strings

**TREMOLO 3**

a *tremolo* on the same pitch

**GLISSANDO**

# WHY PRACTISE TECHNICAL EXERCISES?

The main reason for practising technical exercises is that they will help you play well, in that they will improve your technique. Unfortunately, it is this aspect of playing the violin that will make or break you. If it is any comfort, this is true for all musicians on any instrument.

If you have ever seen a concert violinist do the improbable, the impossible and the downright scary on his or her instrument, then you should know that countless hours of technical exercises have produced that ability. The unfortunate thing is that practising technical exercises can be very boring indeed.

Many people stop playing shortly after they have started because their teachers overemphasize exercises. But teachers do so because they are as important as breathing. I have included a few exercises to get you started. Even so, they should not become an end in themselves. The main reason you are playing the violin is to make music and enjoy yourself. If you want to ignore the technical aspect of playing, then so be it. But it would be a pity not to use the exercises to help you play well. They following exercises are divided into four for the left hand (fingering exercises) and four for the right hand (bowing exercises).

## Exercise 1 – The rest position

Hold the violin in position. Rest your left hand against the body of the violin, so that all four fingers are just above the G-string and the thumb rests in the curve of the neck (the shoulder). Make sure your elbow comes 'in' under the body of the violin and that your left hand is not the main support for the instrument (the shoulder rest should provide enough support). Remember that your wrist should be in line with your arm.

Now pluck the G-string four times with the 4th finger (a). Repeat this exercise on the G-string with each finger (b). You can also try this exercise on the other strings as well. To make it more interesting, alternate fingers (c) or experiment with various rhythms (d) while plucking the strings. This exercise will develop your finger strength and agility as well as getting your left hand used to this (initially uncomfortable) position.

**THE REST POSITION**

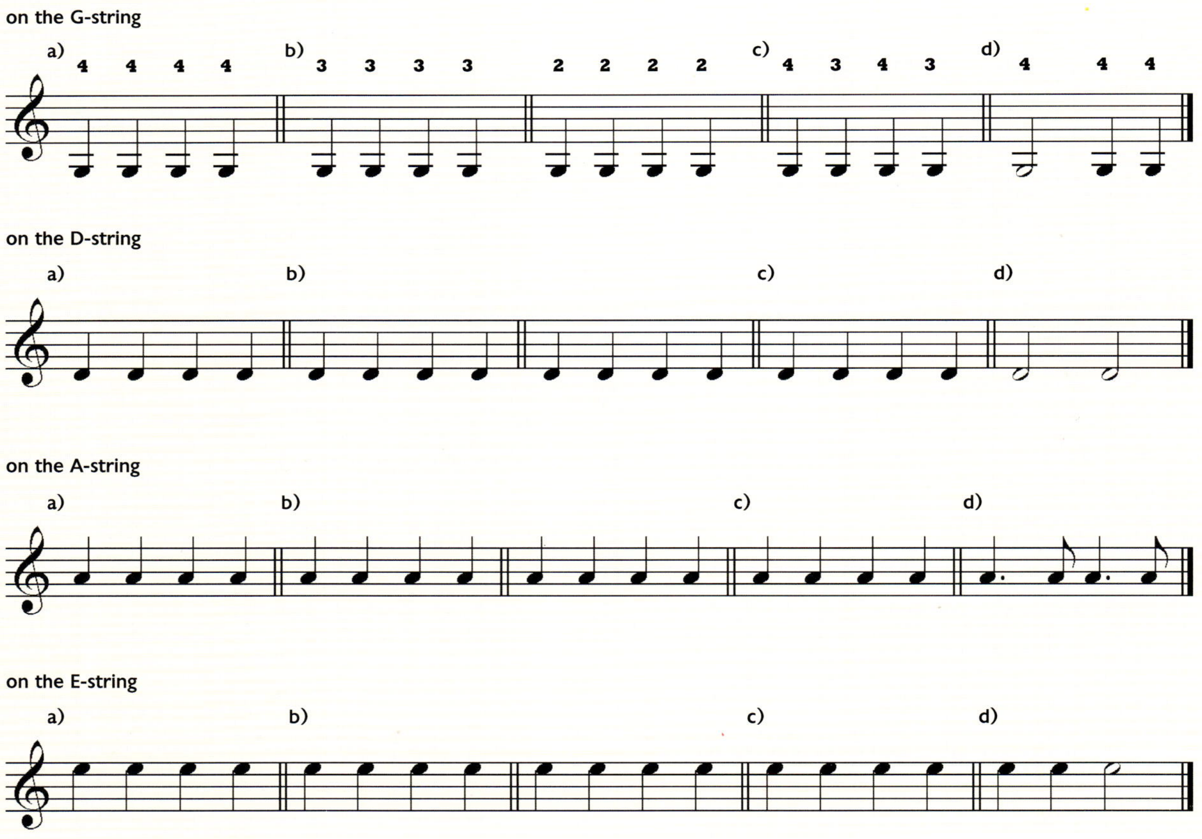

## Exercise 2 – Finger frame 1

Start the exercise on the D-string as indicated. Make sure the note G in bar 3 (played by the 3rd finger), and the note G (on the open G-string) in bar 4, are in tune and an octave apart. Also make sure that the four As in bar 6 are in tune. The string on which the notes should be played is indicated by Roman numerals (the G-string is IV, D is III, A is II and E is I) above the stave. Keep your wrist rounded and the elbow in.

This exercise teaches you the correct distances for the notes in the first finger frame (see p22) and helps to develop your ear so that you recognise notes which are in tune.

**FINGER FRAME I**

**0** refers to an open string

## Exercise 3 – *Mary Had A Little Lamb*

This exercise is indicated on the D-string, but can be played on all the strings. Play the D-string first, then G, then A and finally E. Make sure you keep the thumb of the left hand relaxed. Tap it a few times to loosen it. Also try to keep a small space between your hand and the neck of the violin – perhaps just enough to accommodate a mouse. Check that the A in bar 4 is in tune by playing the open A-string. Obviously, you will not be able to perform this check on the E-string, but since most of us know how *Mary Had A Little Lamb* should sound, this should not be a problem.

**MARY HAD A LITTLE LAMB**

## Exercise 4 – The sliding finger

As you saw with the other finger frames (p39), the fingers have to move around to fill in the 'gaps'. A finger can slide forwards (towards the bridge – indicated by +) or backwards (towards the nut – indicated by -). When sliding a finger, you start by releasing the pressure, but still keeping contact with the string. Now slide the finger slowly and smoothly into its new position and stop the string, making sure that the thumb does not move and stays relaxed. The backward extension of the 1st finger will form a square (the finger scrunches up). This exercise is probably the most important because it helps your fingers feel the distance of a semitone and teaches your ear to hear the distance of a semitone.

**THE SLIDING FINGER**

## Exercise 5 – Bowing the open strings

Start this exercise with a down-bow by placing the bow (near the frog) on the string between the bridge and fingerboard. Make sure the bow is flat (in other words, the width of the ribbon is on the string) and keep the 90-degree angle between bow and string. At the heel, it is necessary for the entire ribbon to be in contact with the strings. Give a full down-bow until you reach the point. When you reach the point, your arm should be straight. Now give an up-bow. Remember to bend your wrist as you get near the frog otherwise your bowing angle will be wrong. Make sure your bowings are long and slow.

By varying the bow pressure you can change the intensity and volume of the note, but the bow should not bounce around on the string. The height of your elbow will change depending on which string you are playing.

**BOWING THE OPEN STRINGS**

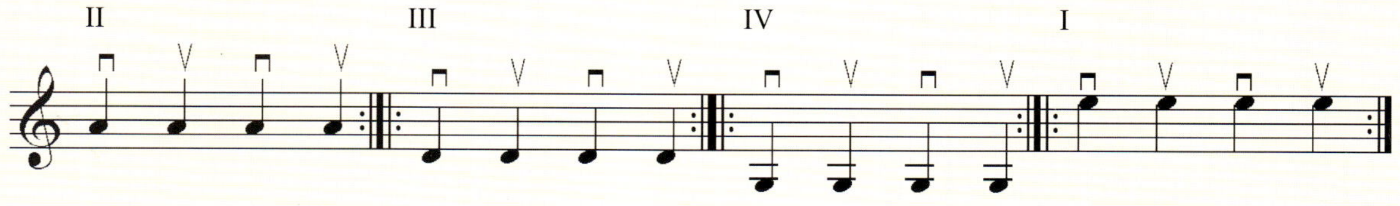

## Exercise 6 – String changing

This exercise must be played very slowly so that you have time to think about every action you have to make. Exercise (a) is explained in full. You should be able to figure the rest out on your own. Start by playing a down-bow on the G-string. When you reach the point, stop. Now lower your elbow and shift the ribbon from the G-string to the D-string without making a sound. Now give an up-bow on the D-string. When you reach the frog, stop again. Lower your elbow and the ribbon onto the A-string (without a sound) and then proceed with another down-bow. Then play the E-string using an up-bow, making sure to go through all the steps.

As you can see, it is quite tricky to concentrate on all the small movements this exercise entails. Remember that the height of your elbow has to change in order to play the different strings comfortably. Now play the other exercises described below.

**STRING CHANGING**

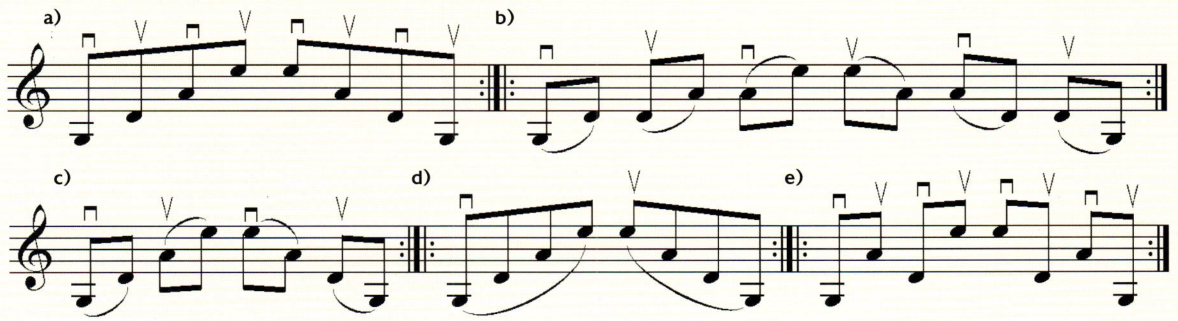


## Exercise 7 – Finger Frames

The finger frame exercises are quite difficult since they mean you have to concentrate on bowing and fingering at the same time. But do not worry. You will get it if you focus on one activity first. Always start by plucking the strings with the right hand, making sure the fingering of the left hand is secure and that the notes are in tune. Once you are sure of the fingering, concentrate on the bowing. Each note must be bowed separately and all notes must utilize the entire bow. This means you have to bow the quarter notes twice as fast as the half notes if you want to use full bows. The two half notes are an octave apart and are to help you check that you are playing in tune. Make sure you have the first finger frame (a) completely under control before moving on to practise the other finger frames.

**FINGER FRAMES**

## Exercise 8 – Bow division

This exercise teaches you how to divide the bow for the different rhythms you play. In the previous exercise, you had to increase the bow speed for the shorter note values. The other way to do this is to vary the 'amount' of bow you use. In this exercise, each quarter note is played with a full bow whereas the eighth notes are played with a half bow.

Start by playing on the open strings (a). When you have mastered the movements, try them with the finger frames demonstrated in Exercise 7 and experiment with the rhythm (b). Make up your own exercises if you feel they will help you master any areas where you may be experiencing difficulty. But remember that these exercises are just guidelines.

**BOW DIVISION**

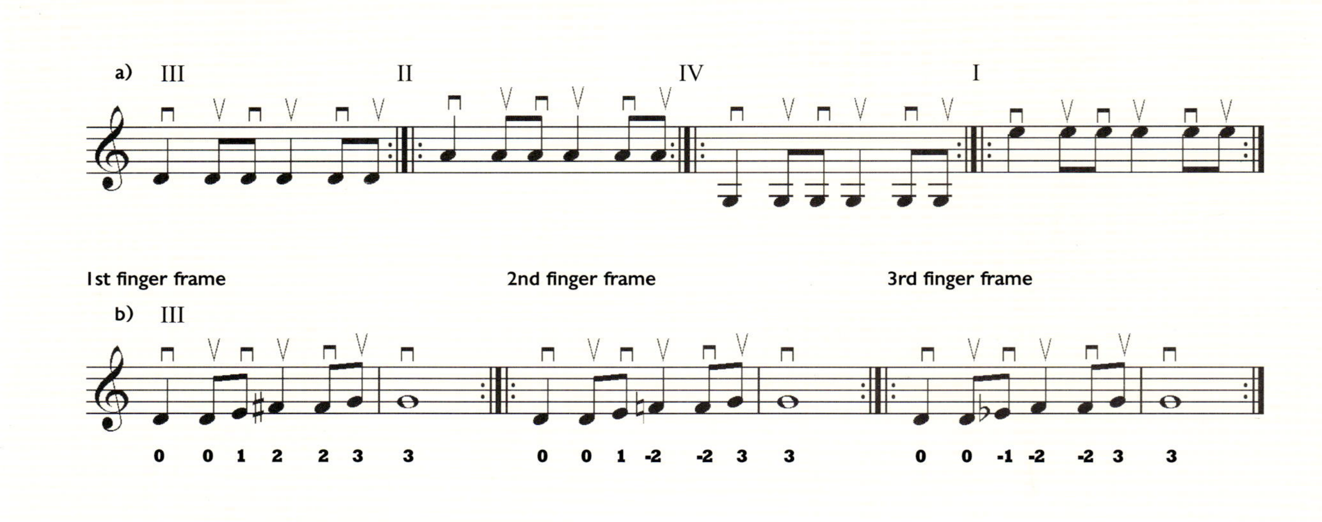

## Some tips for practising

Practising with a purpose will help you achieve results faster than playing in an unsystematic and unfocussed way. Practising should never be a chore, but should be seen as your road towards a certain goal. Try not to become discouraged if things take longer than you thought they would. Learning an instrument, especially one like the violin, takes time. Every musician has to practise and it is the one aspect of playing that teaches you the most about yourself. Are you patient or easily distracted? Are you hardworking or looking for quick results? Would you rather do anything else than practise? Approach your practising with goals in mind and you will find it easier to set aside the necessary time. Structure your practice sessions as you would your exercise regime or going to the gym. These tips will help you focus on what to do when practising. Follow them if you want to, but remember that you are doing this to enjoy yourself. Make your practice sessions enjoyable. Ignore these tips if they hamper your enjoyment in any way.

**LEFT** Although it takes time and patience, practising with a goal in mind will help make your practising sessions more enjoyable.

- Practise using one hand at a time. Start by deciding how you are going to finger the various notes. Practise the fingering by plucking the notes first. Then decide on your bowing. Practise this by bowing all the open strings on which the various notes will be stopped. When you are sure of both fingering and bowing, put them together.
- Once you have chosen the fingering and bowing for a piece, stick to it. Your body 'memorizes' the movements each note needs and changing your fingering and bowing too often will retard your progress. Fingerings and bowings have been included in this book, but are not the only possible options. When you are more adept, you can start choosing your own fingering.
- Start slowly. You are not going to achieve anything by seeing how fast you can play a piece. Once your fingers are secure you can speed up your playing gradually.
- Do not look at your left hand too often. Your fingers should become used to the distances between the notes on the fingerboard. This will leave you free to concentrate on the written music in front of you.
- Divide the piece you are practising into sections and concentrate on one section at a time.
- Never ignore mistakes. Stop and play the section again. Once you have played it perfectly at least five times you can move on.
- Count out loud when you are practising, or get a metronome to help you keep a steady beat while you are playing. Metronomes come in mechanical, electronic and digital varieties and can be bought in any musical instrument shop. Only when you are able to play a piece 'perfectly' in time should you proceed to experiment with its speed and its musicality.
- Before you start a new piece, mark various things that your eyes might miss (see p46) when you are concentrating on the notes and rhythms.
- Even if you are good at memorizing the music, try not to play without the music in front of you. Players who rely too heavily on memory are usually poor sight-readers and this inhibits their ability to learn new pieces or play any music on the spot.

## Putting the violin away

When you have finished practising, don't leave your violin lying around. Rub the body, strings and fingerboard with a soft, dry cloth to remove dust, dirt and rosin and put it back in the case after removing the shoulder rest.

Loosen the ribbon by turning the adjuster and put the bow in its compartment. Most violin cases have a spare compartment where you can put all the various bits like rosin, mutes, spare strings, etc.

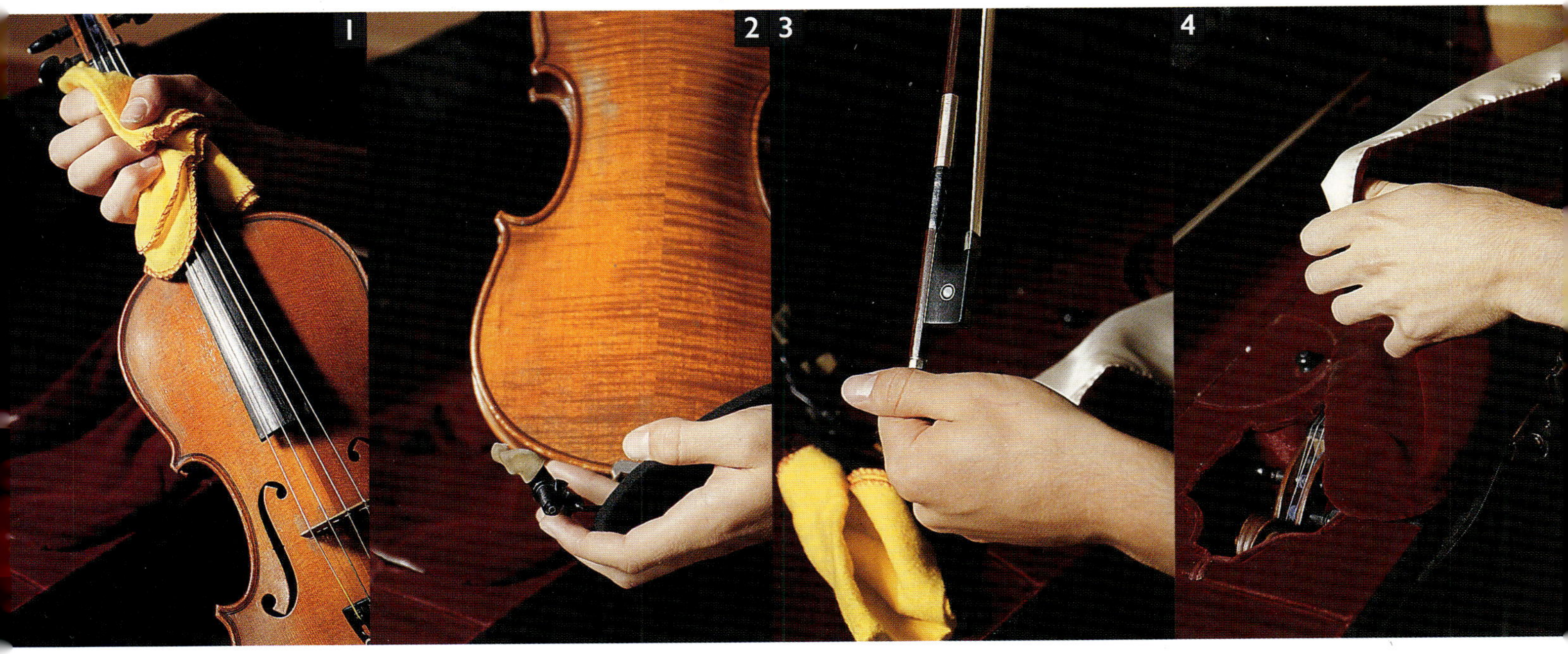


**ABOVE** (1) Wipe the violin with a soft, dry cloth to inhibit dirt and rosin build-up which dulls the sound of the strings.
(2) Remove the shoulder rest, as you will not be able to close the lid of the violin case if it is still on.
(3) Loosen the ribbon after playing to prevent it overstretching while the bow is not being used.
(4) Pack away the violin gently. It is a precious thing and should be looked after properly.

chapter four

# KNOW YOUR MUSIC

INTERPRETATION FORMS ONE OF THE CORNERSTONES of musical performance and is the cause of fiery debates. Interpretation takes place on three levels. The first is an accurate rendition of what the composers wrote. This refers not only to the notes, but also to all the other interpretive bits and bobs, like dynamics and tempo, which the composers added to enhance the emotional character of their work. Some composers, however, especially those before the 18th century, did not give these signs and the interpretation of their music offers some freedom to performers.

The second form of interpretation is a reflection of the stylistic norms and conventions of a certain era. For example, you cannot play Handel in the same manner as you would Honegger. Apart from being different composers, they are from wildly different times and therefore wrote in completely different styles. It is very important to understand the context in which a work was written.

The third aspect of interpretation is deeply personal and differs from player to player. This is why two recordings of the same work by different artists will never sound exactly the same. Consummate players bring their own personality to a work and, in this way, communicate on an emotional level with the composer. This is the goal and makes all the practising worthwhile.

To aid you in interpretation, this chapter contains pieces of music from across a range of 300 years, each piece from a specific time and written in a specific style. Each period is discussed briefly to give some artistic, social and political context to the music and provides some general advice concerning the second level of interpretation. Each piece also includes a short biography introducing the composer, and playing notes, which will navigate you through each piece.

If you are unsure of some of the terms, refer back to chapters 2 and 3 as well as the glossary at the end of the book. As you progress, you will start picking up terms automatically and will have to refer back less and less. Even though some of these pieces might be a bit 'advanced', you should not let that put you off, since you can figure out most things if you are shown the right way to do them.

Enjoy this chapter.

**OPPOSITE** Playing a piece of music establishes a link with the great artistic minds of the past.

## Reading through a piece of music

There are some things you have to do before you even consider picking up your bow, and you will find it best if you go about them systematically. This page contains a good method of deciphering a piece of music before you play it, understanding its mood and preparing yourself mentally to play it. Use the piece illustrated on the opposite page as an example.

First, find out who the composer is and when he lived. The piece opposite was written by Edward Elgar (1857–1934), an Englishman who wrote in a Late Romantic idiom (see p60). Now find out what you can about his life and the time in which he lived, to get some insight into how to interpret his music. Check the head of the page for a work, catalogue or opus number, which specifies the exact work and also gives a clue as to when it was written (usually the smaller the number, the earlier the work). Now run through the rest of the preliminaries as outlined below. Try to memorize the order in which you do all these things, as it will make your preparation more efficient.

### PLAYING NOTES

- Does the title (A) give any clues concerning interpretation? In this case it pretty clearly indicates that the piece is a melodious one for beginners on the violin, to be played at a moderately slow walking pace (*andante*).
- Do you understand the tempo indication (B) and does it remain constant throughout? In this piece it remains constant except for the *ritardando* in bar 23.
- Does the time signature (C) remain constant? Can you spot all the main beats? In this piece, the time signature is constant.
- What is the key signature (D)? Do you know which notes have to be flattened or sharpened? In this case there are no sharps or flat in the key signature, so you play each note as you see it. Also check for accidentals (E). Make sure you know what each note is before you try to play it.
- Check if any sections can be played using only one finger frame and mark them.
- Also scan the work for signs which concern articulation (F). Mark the bowings (G) and fingering you plan to use.
- Scan the piece for dynamic markings (H) and make a mental note of the bow pressure you are going to use to achieve the desired dynamic effect.
- Look for any words which have a bearing on the character of the piece. Make sure you know the meaning of them all before you start. In this piece, there are no such words, but they would include words like *cantabile* and *delicato* (see glossary).

A Andante

No. 1 from *Very Easy Melodious Exercises in the First Position* Op. 22

# BAROQUE MUSIC

Throughout the 17th and first half of the 18th centuries (a time known as the Baroque period), musicians were accorded the same lack of respect as domestic servants. They dressed like servants, ate with servants, slept with servants (probably to make more musicians) and were allowed near nobility only when their musical services were required.

If a musician was not in the service of the aristocracy, he probably worked for the church or the local town council. Even geniuses like Bach, Handel and Mozart had to bow and scrape to curry favour with their employers (although Mozart is famous for his lack of respect in this regard). Despite these humiliating circumstances, musicians found their playing skills in great demand.

Musical rivalry between the different courts of Europe was of great consequence to the world of music. If the coffers were not drained by military campaigns, the nobility made sure they maintained a court orchestra, employed a court composer and, often, even a few singers and dancers. When they weren't fighting or philandering, the aristocrats had little to do, and dancers, singers and musicians were just the thing to keep them sufficiently occupied so that they could forget about the rigours of ruling.

Since Italy was an important centre of musical life in Europe during this time, anything Italian was soon disseminated throughout the continent. The violin was gaining a name for itself and soon found a place in most courts and churches. One of the earliest composers to write substantial chamber works for the violin was Biagio Marini (1594–1663). He utilized many effects which later became common practice, like *tremolo*, multiple-stopping and *scordatura* (see Glossary).

Two of the greatest Italian violinists and, indeed, composers of this time were Arcangelo Corelli (1653–1713) and Antonio Vivaldi (1678–1741), whose numerous violin concertos and *concerti grossi* attest to the dominant role the violin came to fill in this and subsequent eras.

In France, King Louis XIII (1601–43) inherited a fine musical establishment from his father, Henri IV, who commissioned court ballets and dance suites featuring the violin. Louis XIII himself was a competent composer, musician and dancer and established a significant troupe at his court, *Les Vingt-Quatre Violons du Roy* (the 24 Violins of the King), which did much to spread the popularity of the violin.

His son, Louis XIV, also a very enthusiastic and competent dancer, maintained the most extravagant court in Europe at

*Chamber Orchestra for Opera in Venice*, by Marco Ricci, c1710. Italian music was predominant in Europe at the end of the 17th century, and the violin was gaining popularity in the small orchestras that played at the courts.

his palace at Versailles, particularly in the area of the performing arts, and every other monarchy, duchy, electorate and princedom tried to emulate this glorious display. If the French style did not dominate a court then the Italian style did, as Italian instruments were prized above all others.

The difference between the two styles, simplified, is that a composer writing Italian-style music heard singers, whereas when writing French-style music, he saw dancers.

One of the most important French composers of the time was the Florentine Jean-Baptiste Lully (1632–87) who started as a violinist in Louis XIV's court and became its director of music. He brought Italian-style opera to the French court, and adapted it to French taste.

The church also held a great deal of financial and political clout and, as reformation and counter-reformation swept through Europe, made it its mission to maintain the best musical establishment possible to attract worshippers. In this atmosphere many new musical genres developed, like opera, the oratorio (see glossary), sonata and the trio sonata (see p81), which gave a prominent place to the violin.

This was also the time in which virtuosity came to the fore. Castrati (castrated male singers) were considered the rock stars of the time because of their vocal acrobatics and the exorbitant fees they demanded. Soon, instrumentalists and composers were also playing and writing solo concertos and sonatas (see p82) to impress their patrons and congregations with their own brand of musical fireworks.

## SOME BAROQUE COMPOSERS AND THEIR WORKS

**Johann Sebastian Bach (1685–1750)**
6 partitas and sonatas for solo violin, violin concertos and a concerto for 2 violins; Brandenburg Concertos
**Arcangelo Corelli (1653–1713)**
Chamber and church sonatas, 12 *concerti grossi*
**George Frederick Handel (1685–1759)**
Over 45 operas, including *Rinaldo* and *Julius Caesar*; *Saul*; *Messiah*; *concerti grossi*; *Water Music*
**Jean-Baptiste Lully (1632–87)**
30 comedy-ballets, 13 operas and 14 lyrical tragedies
**Antonio Vivaldi (1678–1741)**
40 violin sonatas; 27 trio sonatas; 373 solo concertos, including *Four Seasons* and *Il Cardellino*

## PLAYING NOTES

- Musicologists have been piecing together information on 'early' music for years, but there are still some aspects of interpretation which are a mystery to modern performers. It is this freedom, however, that gives 'early' music its unique appeal.

- Composers of this time did not often indicate tempo, articulation and dynamic signs, since most musicians knew how to play the music.

- Ornaments abound in music from this time. An ornament serves to embellish a melodic line and can be either written down or improvised. The trill (see p37) is one example. The ornament and the note it ornaments should be played in the same time as the main note.

- The balance of the baroque bow meant that the lower half was the more natural place to play. The equivalent for the modern bow is the upper half, so focusing on this half should give the desired effect.

- Vibrato is considered an ornament at this time.

# *Johann Sebastian Bach*

**Johann Sebastian Bach**
1685–1750

Bach was born in the town of Eisenach in what is now Germany, and was orphaned before he was ten. He was raised by his brother, Johann Christoph, under whose guidance he developed an exceptional talent as a keyboard player. Whenever he took part in a competition, the challenger would usually head for the hills. Bach held posts as organist at Mühlhausen and Weimar (where he was also a violinist) and, after a short period of imprisonment (because he wished to be released by his employer, who refused), he became Kapellmeister of the imperial band at Cöthen. Here he wrote many famous orchestral pieces and several concertos for one and two violins.

His growing family (he fathered no less than 20 children) prompted Bach to settle in Leipzig in 1723 where his sons could receive a better education. There he held the post of Cantor (master of church music) until his death in 1750, and was responsible for providing the four churches, the municipality and any festive occasion with music. He finally died of a stroke after a failed operation to remove cataracts.

Shortly after his death, Bach's music fell into relative obscurity. The 'Bach revival' started only in the first half of the 19th century when Mendelssohn performed Bach's *St Matthew Passion* (which left even Nietzsche wondering if there may be a God).

## PLAYING NOTES

- A minuet is a stately French court dance in triple time.
- The tempo is approximately 80 quarter notes per minute.
- This piece has one sharp (F) as a key signature and all Fs should be sharpened unless altered by an accidental like a natural sign or a flat sign. Also notice the C sharps in bars 13 & 16. The C natural in bar 18 is just a cautionary accidental to remind the player that the previous C sharps apply to their respective bars only.
- Bars 1-6: 2nd finger frame (FF) 2; 7-13: 1st FF 1; 14-15: 2nd FF; 16-17: 1st FF; 18-23: 2nd FF; 24-25: 1st FF.
- The // before bar 18 refers to a retake. When you have played the down-bow, 'retake' the bow back to the frog (without touching the string) and play another down-bow. Practise this by resting the bow on the string at the point, and then making a big anti-clockwise movement, bringing the bow to rest on the string at the frog.
- Practise the bowing of bar 1 on the open A-string. The second and third notes use a stopped bow (louré), where you stop the bow halfway, then continue with the up-bow so that both notes are articulated.
- When you play the rhythm in bar 2 with this specific bowing pattern, make sure you play the eighth notes using the upper half of the bow.
- In Baroque music, when repeating a section, the melody is ornamented. A few ornaments have been suggested in the right-hand part of the piano accompaniment.

# Minuet

Johann Sebastian Bach

# George Frederick Handel

Handel was born in Halle, Saxony, in the same year as Bach but, unlike Bach, he was not born into a musical family. Like many composers through the ages, he had a thoroughly obstinate father who insisted on the legal profession for his son. Even after his father's death, he finished his legal studies before pursuing a musical career. He began as a violinist and harpsichordist at the Hamburg opera.

In 1710 he became Kapellmeister to the Elector of Hanover but, after a visit to England in the same year, he settled there permanently in 1712. This proved an embarrassment, since his old employer, who had never dismissed him, soon became his new employer as King George I of England. Luckily, Handel made musical amends with the king by writing his famous orchestral suite, *Water Music* (an excerpt of which is on the opposite page). Handel wrote most of his 40-odd operas in England and later turned to oratorios, of which the *Messiah* is his most famous. Among his many instrumental works are sonatas for violin.

Handel was very aware of the changes in public taste, something Bach ignored altogether. It is a strange coincidence that these musical contemporaries, who never met one another, were also blinded by the same surgeon.

**George Frederick Handel**
1685–1759

## PLAYING NOTES

- A bourrée is also a French dance, but is livelier than a minuet. This specific bourrée comes from the *Water Music* Handel wrote for King George I for a barge party on the Thames.
- The tempo is quite fast and if you are a beginner you will have to content yourself with a slower speed until your playing improves.
- The time signature, which looks like a C with a line running through it, is another way of writing 2/2.
- This piece has a F and C sharp in its key signature.
- You start this piece on an upbeat. Bars 1-4: 1st FF; bars 5-8: 2nd FF; bars 9-16: 1st FF; bars 16-19: 2nd FF; 1st half of bar 20: 1st FF; 2nd half of bar 20-22: 2nd FF; bars 23-24: 1st FF.
- All notes are bowed separately (meaning that the bow direction changes for each note) except where slurs (bars 12, 15, 17, 18, 20 and 23) indicate that two notes should be played in one bowing.
- In the first half of this piece each phrase starts on an up-bow, which means that a retake is necessary in bars 4 and 8. Play the second notes of these phrase endings softer and lighter to give a sense of closure.
- From bar 9 onwards, quarter notes are played using a full bow and eighth notes using a half bow.
- The notes of bars 5-8 and 17-24 are the same as bars 1-4 and 9-16 respectively, merely played an octave higher. These 'repeats' can be played at a softer dynamic level, since dynamic contrasts are typical of music in this style.

# Bourrée

HWV 349/V

**George Frederick Handel**

# CLASSICAL MUSIC

There have been many intellectual movements through the ages. One with particular significance to the world of music was the Enlightenment, which reached its high point in the 18th century. Up until this time, the social structure of Europe was largely religious, in that most artistic activities and social interaction were linked with the church. The other supporter of the arts was the court. The Enlightenment caused a resurgence in humanistic traditions and philosophies, which gave greater prominence to the 'common man' and his place in the universe. The writings of Voltaire, Thomas Paine and Jean-Jacques Rousseau were all-important in shaping these new ideals.

Wolfgang Amadeus Mozart serenades his first love with the violin, in a painting by H Volkmer.

The main supporters of music were still the aristocracy and the church. But the absolute rule of these institutions was being questioned and the middle class started taking over the patronage of the arts. Every rich merchant could commission paintings of his mistress, while paying for elaborate entertainments to celebrate his wedding anniversaries.

Composers were still regarded as servants who had to fulfil their employers' every whim, but the money was running out and the courts were mere shadows of their former glory.

Vienna became the cultural heart of music during this time, a change illustrated by the predominance of the three great Viennese composers, Mozart, Haydn and Beethoven. Mozart wrote music for the church and the court.

Beethoven (1770–1827) was the first freelance composer, who survived financially without relying on the court or church and wrote mostly for wealthy patrons. Much of Mozart's music is very elegant and graceful, to suit his patrons, while Beethoven expressed himself in a more personal musical idiom.

The growth of the more affluent middle classes gave rise to the public concert. These 'subscription' concerts were one of the main cultural activities in Vienna, and Mozart wrote most of his piano concertos for them.

Composers also started expressing themselves in new structures, like the 'Classical' sonata and the symphony, of which Mozart, Haydn and Beethoven were all masters. The violin, which was already established as a popular instrument for composers, now gained further ground as one of the main family of instruments which make up both the symphony orchestra and the string quartet, which also developed in this period.

The Enlightenment emphasized rationality in contrast to emotion, and the educational betterment of individuals. In music it led to a fashion for elegant simplicity and balanced symmetry, which was a direct consequence of renewed interest in the classical civilizations and culture of ancient Greece and Rome. This was one of the reasons this style of music was termed 'Classical' by later generations.

## SOME CLASSICAL COMPOSERS AND THEIR WORKS

**Muzio Clementi (1752–1832)**
*Gradus ad Parnassum* or *Introduction to The Art of Playing on the Piano Forte*; Symphony no. 3 'Great National'; over 100 keyboard sonatas

**Christoph Willibald von Gluck (1714–1787)**
50 operas, including *Artaserse, Ippolito, La Semiramide riconosciuta, La danza, Antigone, Alceste, Orpheus and Eurydice, Echo et Narcisse, Armide* and *Paride ed Elena*

**Joseph Haydn (1732–1801)**
6 oratorios, including *Die Schöpfung* and *Die Jahreszeiten*; over 100 symphonies, including no. 104, 'London', and no. 101 'The Clock'; over 80 string quartets; 9 violin concertos

**Wolfgang Amadeus Mozart (1756–91)**
20 operas, including *Die Zauberflöte* and *Don Giovanni*; 27 string quartets; and concertos for violin

**Ludwig van Beethoven (1770–1827)**
9 symphonies; violin concerto op. 61; 16 string quartets; piano concerto no. 2, op. 19; 3 piano trios op. 1; piano sonatas 1–3, op. 2; string trios op. 9; 24 variations on *Venni amore*, WOO65, for piano

The Rococo and *galant* styles of music echoed the gaiety of the *fête champêtre*, or country party, here painted by Joseph Francis Nollekens, 1702–48.

There are quite a few other musical trends closely associated with the Enlightenment. The description of a piece as 'Rococo' identifies it as lighter than the grandiose and Herculean undertakings of the preceding era. Another musical epithet was *Empfindsamkeit*, which described works of intimate and 'supersensitive' expression. The French *galant* style, closely connected with *Empfindsamkeit*, denotes music which has a pleasing melody, is lightly accompanied and aims to please the sensitive listener. One proponent of this style was CPE Bach (1714–88), the son of JS Bach. The complex structures and textures of the preceding 'church style', which relied heavily on counterpoint (see p94), were simplified to accommodate this new, lighter aesthetic.

The desire to improve society meant that many national theatres developed, which gave impetus to a new range of musical expression like German opera, and *Singspiel* (which combined singing and talking). Realism became important and opera plots, previously elaborate and difficult to follow, became simpler and stressed the human elements in the story. The composer Christoph Willibald von Gluck (1714–87) (see p56) was seen as the great reformer of opera along these lines with his opera *Orpheus and Eurydice*, in 1762. Gluck also modified the style of opera music, which resulted in an increase in the size of the orchestra and created a greater role for violins.

One of the most important secular manifestations of the Enlightenment was Freemasonry, a fraternal movement which originated in the Middle Ages. It derived from the practice of allowing apprentice stonemasons into the lodges of working masons, and evolved into a ritualistic allegory of this practice. The Freemason mental temple is supported by three pillars; namely Nature, Reason and Wisdom. One of Mozart's operas, *Die Zauberflöte*, is a good example of a piece of music conforming to masonic ideals.

It is not surprising that the elegance and order of the era caused a counter-trend to emerge. The foundations were laid for the grandiose emotions and preoccupation with nature and mythology that characterized the artistic endeavours of the 19th century and gave rise to the 'artist'.

## PLAYING NOTES

- In previous centuries, polyphony (multi-voiced writing) dominated and each voice was equally important. Towards the end of the 17th century, music gravitated towards prominent melodies and bass lines. In the Classical style, melody dominates, with the rest of the music fillng a less prominent role.
- In the 18th century, dynamic indications and other interpretive signs became more frequent, but were not as extreme as in the 19th century.

A ticket for a concert at St Mary's Chapel, London, May 1799, depicting a Hogarth engraving of an orchestra which includes harpsichord, viola da gamba, violins, flute and conductor.

# Christoph Willibald von Gluck

Gluck was born in the town of Erasbach in Bohemia (the modern Czech Republic) and, although his father was a forester, he did have an early musical education. He studied logic and mathematics at the University of Prague, where he came into contact with the rich opera and theatre traditions of the city. This prompted him to leave his studies and pursue a compositional career, with a period of study in Italy.

Gluck straddled the Baroque and Classical periods. He was primarily a theatre composer, who wrote operas and ballet music for various imperial and private theatres – much like Handel before him. Handel reportedly said that Gluck knew no more of counterpoint (see p94) than his cook. The words proved auspicious since it was Gluck who wanted to 'divest opera of all its grotesque superfluity which had so long disfigured it'. In his reform of opera, the orchestra and the chorus began to take part in the dramatic development, and the solo parts were reduced. By expanding the role of the orchestra he also paved the way for the greater role of violins.

Gluck spent the last 30 years of his life travelling between Vienna and Paris to supervise the production of various operas.

**Christoph Willibald von Gluck**
1714–87

## PLAYING NOTES

- This dance is actually a ballet from the opera, *Orpheus and Eurydice*. It is a minuet danced by the choir when Orpheus reaches Elysium, home of the blessed spirits, to rescue Eurydice.
- The tempo is *andante* and should be at a comfortable walking pace. The *poco rit(ardando)* in bar 20 means that you have to slow down slightly in this bar, while the *a tempo* in bar 21 means you have to recommence playing at the original speed.
- This is the first piece with a flat (B) in its key signature.
- Bars 1-5: 3rd FF; 6: 2nd FF; 7-11: 3rd FF; 12: 2nd FF; 13-14: 3rd FF; 1st 2 notes of 15: 2nd FF; rest of 15-16: 3rd FF; 19-20: 2nd FF; 21-25: 3rd FF; 26: 2nd FF; 27-28: 3rd FF.
- Bars 17-18 use third position. To achieve this, place your first finger where your third was, when in first position. The edge of the palm, opposite the thumb, should lightly touch the body of the violin. When shifting from one position to another, make sure that the movement is smooth by sliding into the new position. Remember that your thumb must also move up the neck.
- Practise the change between second and fourth finger in bar 19 by repeating the two notes over and over. This will increase the strength of the little finger.
- When practising your bowing separately from fingering, practise the change in pressure of the bow that will facilitate the dynamics.
- There are a few other interpretive signs. *Dolce* means sweetly while *dolcissimo* means very sweetly. Your sound should be *legato* and delicate (soft).

# Dance

from *Orphée et Eurydice*

**Christoph Willibald von Gluck**

# Wolfgang Amadeus Mozart

Mozart was born in Salzburg and was probably one of the most gifted musicians ever. He played a variety of instruments, including violin, viola, organ and harpsichord. His precocious talent was carefully nurtured by his father, Leopold, himself an able court musician. At the age of six, Mozart and his sister were dragged from one place to the next in a series of 'child prodigy' concerts. This popularized the idea of child musicians so that many parents, among them Beethoven's father, would beat their children and lock them up to practise, hoping to achieve the same as Leopold Mozart.

As a teenager, Mozart held a post as master of the court band, but he wanted to take part in the cosmopolitan musical life of Vienna and, after securing his release, he settled there in 1781. However, Mozart found himself in the wrong place at the wrong time and for the rest of his life could not secure a permanent position with the imperial court. Yet it was in Vienna that he wrote some of his most enduring music, like the operas *Don Giovanni* and *Die Zauberflöte*. One of Mozart's greatest contributions to music was his development of the symphony and the sonata, both of which he made more graceful, lyrical and delicate. As an independent musician he wrote music for subscription concerts and private individuals, but this was not enough to free him of financial turmoil and he died in poverty at the age of 35.

**Wolfgang Amadeus Mozart**
1756–91

## PLAYING NOTES

- The title of this piece, which is a transcription of a song by Mozart, can be translated as *Yearning for Spring* and is part of the huge body of works that European composers churned out every year to anticipate spring or celebrate the passing of winter.
- *Allegretto* means slightly less lively than *allegro* (fast and cheerful).
- The time signature is 6/8, which is a compound time signature. Remember that the accent falls on the 1st and 4th beats.
- The key signature has one sharp (F).
- This piece starts on an up-beat (see p94). Bars 1–1st half of 11: 2nd FF; 2nd half of 11: 1st FF; 12–16: 2nd FF.
- Use bar 8 to practise stopping the bow and then restarting the bowing action, moving in the same direction.
- In bars 1, 3, 5 and 7 you have to make use of 'tucked' bowing. This means you have to stop the bow just before the eighth note so that it can also be properly articulated in the same bow.
- This piece requires you to play multiple notes on each bow, so you have to judge the bow speed correctly in order to play all the notes, and you should play the whole piece in a very *legato* manner (as smoothly as possible). I recommend that you spend a lot of time practising the string changes on open strings before you start practising the fingering of this piece.

# Sehnsucht nach dem Frühling

KV 596

**Wolfgang Amadeus Mozart**

# ROMANTICISM

What is an artist? The most logical answer is: someone who creates art. This begs the question: what is art? Today we may regard a certain work by Bach as a work of art, yet this is not how the composer saw his music. The best he probably thought of it was as a job well done, not as a piece of music with any 'artistic' value. Before the 19th century, composers saw themselves as artisans, not artists.

Only after the Enlightenment did composers start writing music for 'art's' sake, hoping that it might be appreciated by future generations. This was because of a surge in historical consciousness in the 19th century, when musicians started taking an interest in performing works from previous eras. (This 'historicism' has even progressed today to the point where most modern composers have to write for posterity, since they will not hear many of their compositions while they are alive because it simply is not profitable for an orchestra to rehearse and play a piece which might not go down well with an audience. )

The philosophy of this time stressed the individual and the emotions, which in the arts encouraged free expression and gave rise to a new sense of self among musicians, which in turn encouraged the idea of the 'artistic temperament'. This was a highly sensitive being, who was not always in touch with the normal, mundane world around him. He communicated with feelings and these feelings were often stormy and violent.

A true virtuoso performer, Niccolò Paganini (1782–1840) knew how to entertain a crowd. (G F Kersting 1830/31).

## PLAYING NOTES

- In previous eras, broad musical conventions made it possible for composers to include only the barest amount of interpretive markings, since most musicians knew what to do. With the rise of the individualistic temperament, the resulting multiplicity of styles forced composers to become more descriptive (and inventive) in this regard. Musicians could not see the notes for the interpretation.

In this sense, the first 'composer-artist' was Beethoven, who was the first composer able to subsist on commissions from wealthy patrons rather than work for 'employers'.

Since composers were now writing to please their own passions, a wider diversity of styles was produced, from the intimate song-like musical forms of Franz Schubert (1797–1828) to the grandiose works of Richard Wagner (1813–83).

The stormy years after the French Revolution (1789–99), which brought the downfall of the monarchy and aristocracy, gave rise to a new class of patron, consisting of a wealthy middle class and displaced aristocrats. They were more than willing to put up with the eccentricities of the artist in return for a piece of sheet music which they could hand down to their children as a family heirloom.

The name given to the artistic philosophy of the time was 'Romanticism'. It was also characterized by a movement 'back to nature', in which artists were inspired by the beauty and

The Handel Festival in London's Crystal Palace, 1865, provided theatricals such as fireworks to the large and expectant crowd.

mystery of nature (such as Mendelssohn's *Hebrides* overture). Mythology and the supernatural, and the tales of chivalry and knightly honour of the Middle Ages (such as Wagner's opera *Tristan and Isolde*) were other popular themes.

The vogue for freedom of expression saw the appearance of innumerable virtuoso performers, who travelled the length and breadth of Europe to thrill and amaze the masses with their impossible instrumental stunts. The violin was ideally suited to this form of showmanship and gave us such artists as the prodigiously talented Italian, Niccolò Paganini (1782–1840). One of his most famous tricks was to play a difficult piece on the violin and then play the same piece three more times, each time cutting one string. It was even rumoured that he had sold his soul to the Devil in return for his amazing capabilities.

The availability of such virtuosi inspired some composers to write numerous longer violin concerti that were not only on a large scale (some lasting close to an hour) but also fiendishly difficult for mere mortals to play.

The Industrial Revolution meant that the population of Europe started gravitating towards the cities. One result of this was that composers now had a much larger ready audience. Huge concert halls were built to provide entertainment for the masses and this inspired composers to write on a grand scale, further increasing the size of the orchestra. Monstrous ensembles were used to play music which made plaster rain down from the ceiling and inspired many cartoons which depicted cannons and heavy artillery in the orchestra. Since musicians were now entertaining the middle class and not the aristocracy, they had to resort to all sorts of shock tactics and other effects to keep their audiences interested.

This was also the time of the rise of the music critic, another 'artist', who kept the population at large informed and opinionated. This would often cause the musical public to divide into two camps, both of which would settle their differences in a manner not unlike soccer hooliganism. There were, for example, progressive musicians like Liszt and Wagner who scoffed at the pedantic classicism of Brahms and Mendelssohn. Tchaikovsky even wrote in his diary: 'I played over the music of that scoundrel Brahms. What a giftless bastard.' The latter, in turn, regarded the former in the same way you would a child having a tantrum.

## SOME ROMANTIC COMPOSERS AND THEIR WORKS

**Johannes Brahms (1833–97)**
Violin sonatas nos. 1, 2 and 3; sextets nos. 1 and 2 for violin, viola and violoncello; Academic Festival Overture, op. 80; Symphony no. 4, op. 98; 3 Intermezzos, op. 117; *Ein Deutsches Requiem*, op. 45

**Frédéric Chopin (1810–49)**
58 mazurkas; 20 nocturnes; 15 polonaises; 17 waltzes; various other pieces including sonatas, rondos, etudes, ballades and scherzos

**Antonín Dvořák (1841–1904)**
Symphony no. 9, *From the New World,* op. 117; violin concerto, op. 53; string quartet no. 12, '*The American,* op. 96

**Felix Mendelssohn (1809–47)**
Violin concerto, op. 64; Symphony no. 4 'Italian', op. 90; piano sonata, op. 105; string quartets and an octet

**Franz Peter Schubert (1797–1828)**
15 string quartets, including *Death and the Maiden*; as well as quintets and an octet; sonatas and sonatinas for piano and violin

**Robert Schumann (1810–56)**
String quartets and trio sonatas; the 'Rhenish' symphony

**Giuseppe Verdi (1813–1901)**
Operas, including *Nabucco, Macbeth, Il Trovatore, Rigoletto, La Traviata, Aïda, Otello, Un Ballo in Maschera* and *Falstaff*

# Johannes Brahms

Brahms was born in Hamburg and also received his first musical education from his father. As a teenager he played the piano in a brothel and was 'rescued' later, during a musical tour, by the violinist Joseph Joachim, to whom he later dedicated his Violin Concerto op. 77. He was introduced to many of the foremost musicians of the day including Liszt, Schumann and Mendelssohn, who heaped praise on the 20-year-old.

Brahms had a fiery temperament and his music had an emotional depth which clearly expressed the emotional values of the time. Yet, unlike Liszt and Berlioz, Brahms did not completely abandon the clear formal structure of the preceding Classicism, and in this respect he is seen as the true successor of Beethoven. The initial praise heaped on his shoulders made him a very hesitant composer. He finished his first symphony 14 years after he started it. He worked mainly as a choral conductor in Hamburg and later in Vienna, where he settled in 1869. His sensitivity to choral sound produced many outstanding works, among them the *German Requiem*, which is a *tour de force* of the Romantic repertoire.

**Johannes Brahms**
1833–97

## PLAYING NOTES

- The title, which can be translated as *Lullaby*, is quite specific regarding the character of the piece. It should be soft and delicate. In order to achieve a soft, delicate, velvety tone, place the bow closer to, or even on, the fingerboard and tilt the bow away from you slightly so that fewer hairs touch the strings.
- The tempo is andante (at a walking pace) and should rather be too slow than too fast.
- The piece has B flat as a key signature.
- Bars 1-8: 3rd FF; 9: 2nd FF; 10-18: 3rd FF.
- Also use this piece to practise bow retakes (which you will find in bars 4, 10 and 14).
- This piece must be played very smoothly (*legato*) so once again you will have to concentrate on bowing and smooth string changing before you tackle the fingering. Remember that your bowing wrist must not become rigid or unbending, but must be kept loose and relaxed.
- The thirty-second notes in bar 17 form an ornament which has been written out. It should be played lightly and delicately, and increasing the bowing speed slightly will help anticipate the quarter note that follows.

# Wiegenlied

Op. 49 No. 4

**Johannes Brahms**

# Niccolò Paganini

Paganini's name is synonymous with the violin and it was his staggering technique that inspired pianists like Liszt to become the 'Paganini of the piano'. Born in Genoa, he received his first musical education from his father, a dockworker and amateur musician. At the age of 12 he was already giving concerts which showed signs of his advanced sense of showmanship. His compositions laid the basis for his flamboyance. Even though they were difficult they were intended to be outlines, to be improvised during their performance so that each concert would sound different. He wrote six violin concertos, of which the first, No. 1, is the most performed, as well as many smaller works for solo violin with orchestral accompaniment.

A passionate individual, he eloped with a girl in 1814, only to be arrested on a charge of abduction, laid by the girl's father. His life was filled with fiery amorous adventures, but no stable marital union. He did have one illegitimate son for whom he seems to have cared deeply since he played many charity concerts to attain a certificate of legitimacy for him from King Carlo Alberto of Turin. Despite many financial disasters, Paganini was said to have made enough money in one year to buy 300kg (660lb) of gold. On his deathbed, he sent away the priest, which caused him to be accused of impiety by the Bishop of Nice, who did not allow him a religious funeral or burial. Paganini's remains were interred only 36 years after his death.

**Niccolò Paganini**
1782–1840

## PLAYING NOTES

- This piece is more challenging than the others in this book, but I have included it because it is one of the most exciting pieces in the violin repertoire and every beginner should have something to aspire to. Note that the time signature changes in bar 13.
- This is the beginning of *Variazioni di Bravura* from *Caprice No. 24*, which literally means 'showy variations'. You will recognize it immediately when you hear it, as other famous composers like Rachmaninoff, Brahms and Andrew Lloyd Webber have used it.
- There are no sharps or flats in the key signature so you must play each note as you see it.
- Finger frames are mixed, so you will probably have some trouble playing this piece, as your fingers have to move around and stretch a lot more than usual.
- Practise the rhythm of the first two notes using 'tucked' bowing (see p58).
- The sixteenth notes can be practised using separate bowing at first. Also practise the notes using different rhythms.
- When repeating a section, alter the dynamics. To play *forte* (loudly), play closer to the bridge with the entire width of the ribbon in contact with the string (a flat bow), with slightly more pressure on the bow and a faster bowing speed. To play *piano* (softly), play closer to the bridge using less width of the ribbon, with less pressure and a slower bowing speed.

# Theme & 1st Variation

from *Variazioni di Bravura* from *Caprice No. 24*

Niccolò Paganini

**Theme**

**Variation I**

# EXPERIMENTS AND NEW SOUNDS

At the end of the 19th century there was a crisis in Western music. The desire of the 'artist-composer' always to write something unique was becoming more and more difficult to implement as the language of music seemed to have completely exhausted all possibilities. No harmonic progression, melody or theme could be written without it reminding someone of something similar.

For this reason composers and performers started experimenting with unorthodox sounds and techniques to expand the boundaries of musical thought and created a multitude of 'isms', such as Impressionism, Expressionism, Serialism and Neo-classicism, among others.

One of the new sounds was polytonality, in which music is played in more than one key simultaneously. The result is often discordant and harsh. Many composers of the time followed this style, including the Swiss composer Arthur Honegger (1892–1955), a member of the Paris Six who exploited the shock value of dissonance (see p94). Another was Maurice Ravel (1875–1937), whose 1922 *Duo for Violin and Cello* was written with different key signatures for the two instruments in some passages.

The late 19th century produced a new musical vocabulary and a new way of listening to music. One of the Impressionist musicians was Claude Debussy (1862–1918),

Béla Bartók at the Institute of Folklore, Bucharest, in 1934, listening to recordings he made of East European folk music, reflecting an interest in national sounds and rhythms.

The avant-garde American composer Lou Harrison (b.1917) at Dartington Summer School, 1996, with gamelan players.

who experimented with harmonic sequences and the texture and tone colour of music, as in his work *La Mer*. Some of his more revolutionary music was influenced by Javanese gamelan music and Far Eastern sounds, reflecting an interest at the time in the culture of the Orient.

The search for musical alternatives coincided with a growing nationalism, in Europe as well as in the USA. This in turn increased the interest in local sounds and folk music. The English composer Ralph Vaughan Williams (1872–1968), and Hungarians Béla Bartók (1881–1945) and Zoltán Kodály (1882–1967) were among the keenest researchers of folk sounds. Bartók and Kodály travelled through the countryside with a phonograph to record peasant musicians in Hungary, Slovakia and Romania, and in the process discovered ancient Magyar rhythms and modes, which they incorporated into their own works, such as Bartók's *Romanian Folkdances* for violin and piano. The American Aaron Copland (1900–90) worked Appalachian folk songs and even cowboy tunes into his compositions, such as *Rodeo* and *Billy the Kid*.

Atonality was another style which developed at this time, and saw all 12 semitones in the octave as equally important. This seeming anarchy of sound is found particularly in pieces by the German composer Arnold Schoenberg (1874–1951). His compositions exemplified the '12-tone method', in which the 12 notes of the chromatic scale are used as the main compositional element without any regard to key, and with no dominant or leading note (*see* Tonalism, p94). This atonal style had a parallel in Expressionism which was a significant movement in art and theatre at the time.

Schoenberg's 12-tone arrangements, which he applied solely to pitch, were further developed and applied to other elements in music by followers, such as Olivier Messiaen (1908–92), who was inspired by the study of bird songs and by Indian music, creating – despite the rigorous arrangements – an even more chaotic sound.

New electronic instruments were being invented at the time, which lent their sound to 'chance music'. In the USA, Charles Ives (1874–1954) was experimenting with chance, or 'aleatoric' music. Ives, in turn, influenced John Cage (1912–92), who introduced random factors, such as the throw of a dice, into his compositions (although Mozart had done the same thing 200 years earlier).

These experiments alienated a large part of the public, and even composers themselves, since much of the music they produced was strange and not always too pleasant on the ear. This is especially true of the violin which, to some ears, sounds like cats fighting and spitting at one another.

Music seemed to become more and more intellectual. In reaction to this, many composers returned to their classical roots (producing a style termed Neo-classical) and even further back in history. The Russian composer Igor Stravinsky, for example, based his ballet *Pulcinella* on music ascribed to the 18th-century composer Pergolesi. And the English composer Sir Peter Maxwell Davies (b.1934) used medieval rhythm and counterpoint as part of his technique.

Other composers reacted to the intellectualism of the new music by incorporating the more popular sounds of the time, such as jazz and the songs of Irving Berlin. Among them were Erik Satie (1866–1925), Ravel and Shostakovich (1906–75).

The lack of contemporary classical music which was easy to listen to meant that the time was ripe for the sounds of blues, jazz and rock and roll to take over and become the main forms of modern musical entertainment.

## SELECTED 19TH AND 20TH CENTURY COMPOSERS AND THEIR WORKS

**Samuel Barber (1910–81)**
Op.1, *Serenade*, for string quartet; *Adagio for Strings* (1936); Violin concerto (1939)

**Béla Bartók (1881–1945)**
*Concerto for Orchestra; Music for Strings, Percussion and Celesta; Bluebeard's Castle*; Piano concerto no. 1 BB 91

**Benjamin Britten (1913–76)**
*Peter Grimes* op.33; radio music for *King Arthur* and *The Rescue; The Young Person's Guide to the Orchestra*, op .34

**John Cage (1912–92)**
4'33" (Silence); Sonatas and Interludes for Prepared Piano; *Music of Changes; First Construction* for 6 players

**Aaron Copland (1900–1990)**
*Billy the Kid, Rodeo* and *Appalachian Spring; Music for a Great City* (1964); *Stomp Your Foot* for choir (1943); 2 pieces for string quartet

**Claude Debussy (1862–1918)**
*La Mer* (1903-5); *Prélude à l'après-midi d'un faune* (1895); *Pelléas et Mélisande* (1893–1902); *Images* (1908) for piano

**Philip Glass (b.1937)**
*Einstein on the Beach* (1975–6); *Akhnaten* (1983); Violin concerto (1987); *Monsters of Grace* (1998); *Music with changing parts* (1970); Music for *The Hours* (2002)

**Paul Hindemith (1895–1963)**
*Das Nusch-Nuschi*, op. 20; *Mörder*, op. 12; Kammermusik no. 1–7; Symphony, *Mathis der Mahler*

**Sergei Rachmaninoff (1873–1943)**
Piano concerto no .2, op. 18; Symphony no. 2, op. 27; *Moments musicaux*, op. 16; *Etudes tableaux*, op. 33

**Arnold Schoenberg (1874–1951)**
*Pierrot Lunaire; Verklärte Nacht*, op. 4; string quartet no. 3; 5 Klavierstücke, op. 23; Kammersymphonie no. 2, op. 38

**Dmitri Shostakovich (1906–75)**
15 symphonies; 15 string quartets; Violin concerto no. 1, op. 77; Cello concerto no. 1, op. 107; 30 film scores

**Karlheinz Stockhausen (b.1928)**
*Licht* (The Seven Days of the Week); Klavierstucke I-IV no. 2; Kontakte no. 12; Mikrofonie I no. 15 and II no. 17

**Igor Stravinsky (1882–1971)**
String quartet, *Three Pieces* (1914); *Concertino* (1920); ballets, including *The Firebird* (1909–10), *The Rite of Spring* (191–3) and *Petrushka* (1910–11); *Oedipus Rex* (1926–7); *Circus Polka* (1942)

# Béla Bartók

**Béla Bartók**
1881–1945

Bartók was born in the Hungarian province of Torontál. His parents were both teachers and enthusiastic amateur musicians. After some initial lessons in which he excelled, he went to study piano and composition at the Liszt Academy in Budapest. Initially he attracted more interest as a pianist than as a composer and, after a concert tour, he settled as a member of the piano staff of the academy.

He became acquainted with the ethnomusicologist, Zóltan Kodály, and developed a huge interest in the folk music of his native Hungary, Romania and surrounding countries. Between them they collected and transcribed thousands of folk melodies, something that would benefit their compositional language. After the collapse of the Austro-Hungarian Empire, the leftist political agenda initially accused Bartók of treason because of his love for Romanian music, but as time progressed, he became respected and by his fiftieth birthday he could not move for all the rewards and accolades. Fearing Nazi domination, Bartók started shipping his musical scores to Switzerland and the USA, but would not leave until after the death of his mother in 1939. He settled in the USA in 1940, but the war meant that financial security could not be obtained, despite the efforts of well-wishers. Never in robust health since childhood, Bartók finally died from a blood and lung illness.

## PLAYING NOTES

- The title of this piece is quite specific and when you hear it you will picture a lively East European folk dance.
- The piece begins with the tempo indication, *allegro*, but goes through quite a few changes (*calando*, *a tempo*, and *poco ritardando* – see the Glossary.
- The time signature has two beats per bar. Note that an accent often falls on the usually unaccented second beat.
- There are no sharps or flats in the key signature, so play each note as it occurs.
- Bars 1-6: 2nd FF; 7-14: 1st FF; 15-16: 2nd FF; 17-26: 1st FF.
- This piece can be divided into sections of four bars each. The first and last sections are a prelude and postlude for the accompanist. Sections 2 and 4 are the same and sections 3 and 5 are the same, the variation being in the accompaniment. Bars 13 and 14 are an interlude for the accompanist.
- There are many interpretive and articulation markings. To avoid confusion, only bars 5-8 have bowing markings, but these apply to all subsequent sections.
- To play the accented up-bow on the second beat of bars 7, 8 and 11, stop the bow for a second to allow you to 'grip' the string better. Then release the pressure as soon as the bow starts moving and change your bowing speed from fast to slow.

# Dance

from *For Children* Vol. 2

**Béla Bartók**

# Dmitri Shostakovich

While other composers wrote for kings, patrons and the public, Shostakovich's works sometimes appear to have been composed for political ideologies. Soviet Russia influenced him in deeply and his relationship to the ideals of the Soviet regime is one of the most fiercely debated topics in modern musicology. It is perhaps ironic that his grandfather was implicated in the 1866 assassination attempt on Tsar Alexander II.

Shostakovich came from a privileged family and initially had to be persuaded to play the piano. His talent soon blossomed and he became a student at the Petrograd Conservatory where, despite ill health, he finished his education, even playing his final piano exam with a bandaged neck. After the revolution, and the death of his father, he found himself in dire financial straits and, in order to support his mother, started composing music and playing the piano in cinemas to accompany silent films.

A remarkable pianist, sight-reader and memorizer, he was rocketed into stardom by the success of his first symphony and is regarded as one of the best symphonists of the first half of the 20th century. He fought a lifelong battle against critics on both ideological and political grounds. Yet, when he died, many observed him to be the brightest light in the Russian musical firmament.

**Dmitri Shostakovich**
1906–75

## PLAYING NOTES

- The title is rather obvious when it comes to defining the character of this piece. You cannot play a march in the same style as you play a waltz or a lullaby. Therefore, play with fairly fast bow strokes, making sure each note is articulated cleanly and properly.
- The tempo indication also asks for this character.
- The time signature is the crossed C, which means 2/2. Marches are famous for having only two beats per bar, so the first and third quarter notes in each bar should be slightly accented. These 'natural' accents should often be 'thought' rather than played, but the beginner must become acutely aware of where these accents fall (see p20), and accenting the actual notes helpes to enforce this mental picture.
- Remember to sharpen all F's, C's and G's.
- All notes are bowed separately except for the slurred eighth notes. To play accents, put pressure on the bow so that it 'grips' the string and then move it very fast, slowing down immediately. Pressure on the string can be released as soon as the bow has started moving to avoid squeaking or scratching sounds.
- Practise increasing and releasing bow pressure on the strings for playing the crescendi and diminuendi in bars 8, 12, 15, 16 and 20. Also become aware of the difference in required bow pressure for playing different dynamic levels like *mezzo piano* (mp – bar 1) and *forte* (f – bar 9).

# Little March

from *Six Children's Pieces*

**Dmitri Shostakovich**

# MUSIC AND THE MASSES

The 20th century was the most prolific period in the history of music, and what gave it a significant boost were two 19th century inventions, the phonograph and the radio.

Thanks to these, not only was it possible to preserve music indefinitely and record previously unheard-of music from around the world, but music could be communicated simultaneously to many more people than ever before. The two inventions were the most important factors in the spread of styles like blues, jazz, rock and roll, and country music, and they opened the floodgates to pop music.

Jazz and blues evolved from American slave songs and tunes, which in themselves had African roots. The traditional African religions practised by the slaves, characterized by dancing, vigorous percussion, hand-clapping and song, were restrained by conversion to the Christian church, but a version of their expression remained, laying the foundations for spirituals and gospel music. The music mixed the sacred and secular, using euphemism to voice the slaves' fears, concerns and distress, and evolved into a musical style which became known as the blues.

The fiddle, or violin, is a feature of traditional music played in many village pubs in Ireland and the world over.

At the beginning of the 20th century, a more optimistic style was developing in and around New Orleans. Called jazz, it took over and developed the melodic and harmonic elements of blues and introduced a radically new approach to rhythm, which included ample use of syncopation (see p94) and improvisation, a characteristic of African music.

The French musician Stephane Grappelli made the violin his own and his name is now synonymous with jazz violin.

Although jazz and blues were associated with sex, bars and loose morals in general, the development of the Big Band and Swing styles gave them a sense of respectability, and it became possible to hear them in the same concert hall where you would go to hear a violin concerto by Brahms.

Violin was not used extensively in these new sounds, but when it was it certainly made itself heard. One of the greatest exponents of jazz violin was Frenchman Stephane Grappelli (1908–97) who, together with jazz guitarist Django Reinhardt, led the Quintet of the Hot Club of France from 1934–39. A self-taught violinist, Grappelli evolved a unique sound that was lyrical and flowing but with a lively swing.

In the 1950s, the blues combined with country music and developed into rock and roll, which formed the basis for most subsequent forms of popular music.

By the 1990s, performers such as Vanessa Mae and Nigel Kennedy were using the violin to develop a pop sound which derives from a classical base,. A few singers, such as Elvis Costello and Björk, teamed up with string groups like the Brodksy Quartet to create a new sound but, on the whole, the guitar, bass and drums are the instruments of pop.

Irish group The Corrs use traditional instruments, such as the fiddle, bodhran and pipes, to bring a folk edge to their contemporary sound. Sharon Corr is the violinist.

## PLAYING NOTES

- Much Celtic and traditional music has a rapid but smooth-flowing eighth-note movement, in *alla breve* time (see p94), d=120, with two beats to the bar instead of four, i.e. twice as fast as it is written.
- Bow strokes are generally short and light.
- It is usually played in keys of one or two sharps, occasionally three, and falls within two octaves.
- The fiddle can be tuned up or down to make the tune more pleasant to the ear.
- A reel is a fast, forward-moving piece in 4/4 rhythm.

One popular area in which the violin has remained a key instrument, however, is in folk or country music, where it is referred to as the fiddle, even though it is the same thing. The violin started out as a 'folk' instrument and even when it was taken up in the chamber or symphony orchestra, violinists who played at court would often supplement their income by playing at weddings, town festivals and other secular gatherings, and even on the battlefield.

Traditional fiddle musicians distinguish their music and style of playing from that associated with the violin. In Celtic music the fiddle is usually used to play very fast dance tunes, such as the reel, jig and hornpipe, which are characterized by being in two parts, one lower in pitch, followed by a higher part, each with an equal number of bars and played in a variety of contrasting and repeated patterns. The fiddle is particularly significant in Irish and Scottish music, and in the music that was taken to North America and Australia by immigrants.

The violin retains its folk origins in the form of the fiddle, which is a key instrument in country and bluegrass music.

The ballads and dance tunes taken to North America from the early 1600s form the roots of American traditional music, and, since many of the immigrants who imported them worked in rural areas, such as the Appalachians, the music became known as 'mountain' or 'country' music. In fact, the Scottish eightsome reel is the basis of the square dance, or hoedown, in the USA.

The fiddle is part of the distinctive sound of a relatively recent and very popular form of American country music, bluegrass. The name derives from the band, Bill Monroe and the Blue Grass Boys (Monroe came from Kentucky, the Bluegrass State), formed in the late 1930s, and describes a style which incorporates the sound of string bands, gospel, work songs and blues music.

Contemporary composers and songwriters continue to absorb different musical traditions from various parts of the world, creating new and exciting sounds. In the emerging global village, this sublime variety of styles, which is brought to us on CD, radio, TV and mp3, in our cars, offices, living rooms and recreation space, can be explored easily by anyone who has an interest in this universal art form.

# George Gershwin

If anyone straddles the border between popular and serious music it is George Gershwin. The second of four children born to Russian immigrants, George was a troublesome student who once said 'I really like to spend my time with the boys, making somewhat of a nuisance of myself in the streets.' He discovered music by accident, at a penny arcade on Coney Island, when he put some money into a mechanical piano, heard Rubinstein's *Melody in F*, and was transfixed. Aged 15, he dropped out of school and joined a music publisher, working as a song-plugger – a pianist who played to customers to sell them sheet music. His own compositions showed the influence of Irving Berlin, Shostakovich, Debussy, jazz and Jewish chant.

He travelled the vaudeville circuit as a pianist, was hired to write songs and toured as an accompanist. In 1919 Al Jolson heard Gershwin's song *Swanee*, added it to his repertoire, and it became a hit, selling over two million copies in its first year. With his brother Ira, he wrote musicals, but he also wrote serious music, and in 1924 unveiled the piano concerto *Rhapsody in Blue* to rapturous applause. In 1935 his 'folk opera' *Porgy and Bess* was staged, a musical which has since claimed the status of art music although its tunes sit happily in the camp of popular song. In 1937 he fell into a coma and a brain tumour was diagnosed. Two days later he died.

**George Gershwin**
1898–1937

## PLAYING NOTES

- This song is sung by a slave to her baby, in which she lulls the child to sleep by imagining their circumstances to be much better than they are.
- Play this piece in a 'lazy' way to mirror the sultry summer weather of the Southern USA. This can be achieved by making your bow-changes as smooth as possible.
- There are no indicated changes in tempo, but this does not mean that you should play this soulful piece of music like a robot. Just make sure that your accompanist follows you.
- There is no change in the time signature.
- Flatten all Bs and Es.
- The entire piece utilizes the 3rd finger frame.
- In bar 9, make the first C short, as you are illustrating that 'fish are jumpin'.
- In bar 10, keep the first and third fingers down so that you can concentrate on the string changes.
- In bars 16-18, use the upper half of the bow to achieve a gentle sound, since you are playing 'so hush little baby'. When playing an instrumental arrangement of a song, find out the words of the song so that you can mirror its mood.
- The semicircle with a dot, written above the last chord, is called a fermata. This is a pause, but when it occurs at the end of a piece, hold the note until it dies away.

# Summertime

from *Porgy and Bess*

**George Gershwin**
**Arranged by Philip du Toit**

# Fiddles and Folk

The Chieftains

The word 'fiddle' is a generic term for any bowed string instrument, but refers colloquially to a violin played as a folk instrument. There is essentially no difference between the two – except in the way they are played. The fiddle is used to play 'folk' or 'traditional' music, often of Celtic origins, and frequently for fast dance tunes, such as reels, jigs and hornpipes. Few players of traditional music refer to the instrument as a violin. 'Folk' describes music of a common cultural heritage passed on by oral tradition, which does not fall into the 'classical' category and where the composer is often anonymous. This sort of music was traditionally played at festivals, for certain celebrations, such as weddings, and in battle.

The violin/fiddle is such a wonderfully versatile instrument that it is equally at home in popular and classical settings. It is recommended that you expose yourself to fiddle music as well when you are learning to play the instrument because it will add to your understanding of classical music (which often draws on folk sounds) as well as open up new musical vistas for you to explore.

## PLAYING NOTES

- The composer of a traditional tune is often unknown. This is not because he was particularly mediocre, but rather because his tune was learned by memory and handed down from generation to generation, only to be written down centuries later. In these cases, the space where you would look for the composer's name contains 'Anon', or 'Traditional', or the country of origin, as is the case here.
- The titles of traditional pieces are also often quite obscure, but in the first case, the 'Reel' indicates a dance that is of Scottish or Gaelic origin and contains a repetitive pattern or 'travelling figure'. In this case it is the four consecutive eighth notes. The second piece probably refers to a battle.
- It is highly unlikely that the tempo indications of a traditional piece are original. They are usually supplied by the editor.
- Both pieces are in 4/4 time.
- The first piece has one sharp (F) in its key signature and the second piece has two (F and C).
- Each piece is divided into two sections, each of which is repeated.
- First piece: Bar 1: 1st FF; 2: 2nd FF; Bars 3-5: 1st FF; Bars 6-11: 2nd FF; Bars 12-14: 1st FF; Bars 15-16: 2nd FF.
- Second piece: 1st FF throughout.
- It is not unusual for pieces like these to be repeated over and over with slight variations and for each repetition to be played slightly faster until a frenetic pace is achieved.

# Scollay's Reel

# The Silver Spear

chapter five

# DEVELOPING YOUR LISTENING SKILLS

WHEN EXPLAINING HIS WAY OUT OF A SPEEDING TICKET, the conductor, Oscar Levant, allegedly exclaimed: 'You cannot expect me to listen to Beethoven's Ninth and go slow.' Listening to music affects us in various ways and is one of the greatest pleasures in life. Its power has been shown in various studies. In one experiment, music by Beethoven caused a school of fish in an aquarium to change their swimming pattern. In another, pupils who listened to music by Bach and Mozart during periods of study did better in their exams. Even shopping centres have begun to play certain types of music to induce shoppers to spend more.

We listen to music in two ways – passively and actively. Passive listening takes place when the music is not your main concern, but you would notice if it stopped. In an action movie, although your focus is on the hero jumping one train-carriage to another, if this happened in silence it would lose all sense of drama. Active listening, on the other hand, puts the music first.

But why does music give us pleasure? One reason is familiarity. The first time you hear a popular song on the radio, it often does not elicit any emotion from you. However, if you hear the song a second or third time you start remembering the melody. After a few more times you start singing the words and before you realize it, it has become one of your favourite songs. It is familiarity with a piece or song which increases your enjoyment of it, so do not judge a piece of music too harshly the first time you hear it.

Listening pleasure also increases when we are capable of distinguishing one style or genre (type) of music from another. This is especially true with classical music. Being able to distinguish a concerto from a sonata and having a rough knowledge of musical form means that not everything will be unexpected when you listen to a piece of music for the first time. This creates another kind of 'familiarity', which makes new music more accessible.

Since most violin music is classical, it is essential for the budding violinist to take an interest in its forms. To help you, this chapter gives a brief survey of the main types of violin music. It also gives some tips concerning concert protocol – leaving you free of anxiety and able to enjoy the music. Lastly, it suggests a short list of musical pieces worth having in your collection.

**OPPOSITE** It will help your listening skills immeasurably if you treat yourself regularly to live classical concerts where you can watch the violinists play.

# TYPES OF VIOLIN MUSIC

Apart from the piano, the violin has been probably the most favoured instrument by composers through the ages. Consequently, a staggering amount of music has been written for it. The development of orchestral music and the popularity of the violin family in the 18th century meant that the violin was in the right place at the right time to establish itself as the predominant force in the orchestra. Even though it is very difficult to pigeonhole something as subtle and complex as music, compositions featuring the violin can be divided, broadly, into four categories: orchestral music, chamber or ensemble music, works for violin and accompaniment, and works for solo violin.

## Orchestral music

One of the defining characteristics of an orchestra is that it is based on the violin family, which is divided into sections - namely, first violins, second violins, violas, cellos and double basses (which are not, strictly speaking, members of the violin family, as they have flat backs, making them viols).

The orchestra is seated around the conductor. Each section usually plays in unison (meaning they play the same notes). Early orchestras are often referred to as chamber orchestras, because they have fewer types of instruments, and fewer people playing the same notes, than symphony orchestras.

The reason why the modern orchestra is often referred to as a symphony orchestra is because its larger format became standardized in the Classical era, when the symphony was developed. A symphony is a multi-movement work, usually consisting of four contrasting movements (often, fast-slow-minuet/scherzo and trio-fast). Most music for orchestra is referred to as symphonic music and the symphony is the most important type of music written for the orchestra.

Other genres for orchestra include the symphonic poem (a form of 'programme music' – see p82) and the concerto, a work written for soloist and orchestra. The name of the concerto will usually specify the instrument for which it was written, e.g. Mozart's Violin Concerto in A major KV 219. Classical concertos are usually in three movements (fast-slow-fast). The orchestra has also been the composer's first choice for accompanying ballets and works for vocal soloists and choirs, like operas, oratorios, masses and cantatas.

**BELOW** In a symphony orchestra, the violin section, made up of violins, violas and cellos, features prominently.

## Chamber music

Chamber music is played by a varying number of soloists who each play their own separate part of music and do not need a conductor to keep them together. Many see 12 people as the limit, but there are always exceptions. The popularity of the violin as a chamber instrument dates from the early days of consort playing in the 16th century.

There are several chamber combinations which feature the violin, among the most important being the trio sonata, which was popular during the Baroque period. It was written for two melodic instruments (such as the violin and flute, oboe (or recorder) and basso continuo (a sustaining bass instrument, like a cello or bassoon), and one instrument to 'fill' in the chords, like a guitar, lute, harpsichord or organ. It is called a trio sonata because the two players who play the basso continuo act as one. Another important chamber combination is the string quartet. It developed in the Classical era and has been a favourite of composers ever since. It consists of 1st and 2nd violin, viola and cello. Various other combinations include trios (three players), quintets (five), septets (seven) and octets (eight players).

**ABOVE** (1) Many soloists perform first with an accompanist before they play with an orchestra.
(2) The 'classic' piano trio consists of piano, violin and cello.
(3) A string trio can have many different combinations, including two or three of the same instrument.
(4) The string quartet was a very popular ensemble format in the late 18th and early 19th centuries and consists of two violins, a viola and a cello.
(5) This 'reduced' orchestra contains all the main groups of strings, including the large double bass on the far right.

Yehudi Menuhin (1916–99), one of the great solo violinists, plays here c.1969 at the Royal Festival Hall, London.

## Solo violin with accompaniment

Apart from the orchestra, the violin is most often accompanied by a keyboard instrument like the piano. Works for violin and piano accompaniment can be divided into three categories: a specific musical form, such as the sonata; a work with a descriptive title; or a work with some form of technical exercise as its function.

The first includes pieces like rondos (where the main theme A alternates with secondary, contrasting themes B & C and often follows the pattern ABACA); theme and variations (where a recognizable theme is played and then varied in a number of ways); fugues (a type of counterpoint where a theme is stated in one voice and then repeated and imitated by a succession of other voices); and sonatas.

The sonata is probably the most significant genre in this category. It obtained its name from the Italian *suonare*, which refers to music which is played as opposed to being sung (*cantata*). It is a multi-movement work, usually consisting of three movements (fast-slow-fast). The first movement is usually in three-part 'sonata-form': a main and secondary theme are stated in the first part (the exposition); they are altered and developed in the second part (the development); the exposition is restated with minor alterations in the third part (the recapitulation).

Works with descriptive titles are often referred to as programme music. They are usually inspired by non-musical things like nature, lovers or wine, and serve to convey the composer's emotional (if somewhat inebriated) reaction to them. Programme music has been around for a long time, but became especially important in Romantic music in the 19th century. Generic titles include polonaises (Polish dances) and nocturnes (night scenes), but the titles can also be quite specific, like Kinderszenen (children scenes). Although non-musical things are usually an inspiration during composition, an instrumental work is considered to be programme music only if the composer himself gave the piece a descriptive title.

The last category concerns works written to enhance a specific technical aspect of playing the violin. These include toccatas (touch pieces) and études (studies). But just because a piece has a teaching function, it is not necessarily of mediocre quality. Many such pieces are beautiful and exciting even though they were originally written as exercises.

## Solo violin without accompaniment

Since the violin is considered a melodic instrument, most composers wrote works which expect the violin to play just one note at a time. Music for solo violin, however, requires more than just a melody if it is to succeed musically and demands that the violinist play his or her own accompaniment in the form of chords.

Chords are the sound of two or more notes played at the same time and, since violins have four strings with different pitches, it should be possible to play chords on them. When playing two notes simultaneously on adjacent strings, the violinist performs a double-stop. Three notes played together on three adjacent strings are called a triple-stop. Because of the curve in the bridge, it is not possible to play the four notes of a quadruple-stop simultaneously with a modern bow, but this is solved by arpeggiating the chord (playing the notes separately in fast succession). These 'stops' are fiendishly difficult to play in tune and take many years of patient practice to master, which is why most pieces for solo violin are considered difficult. But if a composer has done a good job, the beauty of the music should make up for the fact that it will take you much longer to learn to play it.

# ATTENDING A CONCERT

Before the advent of the radio, television and recordings, live concerts and recitals were the only way of hearing music. Nowadays, pop concerts are eagerly attended by those who relish the opportunity to express, with abandon, their feelings about the performer. But this is not always the case with jazz and classical concerts, where the more rigid rules and conventions can discourage many would-be enthusiasts from attending. This is a great pity, because you can never quite capture on CD the energy of a live performance. For the true audiophile, the live classical concert is also the best place to experience true high-fidelity sound.

Mindful of the traditional formality of concerts, classical musicians have brought themselves up to date. Many established venues are now attracting crowds by offering a relaxed atmosphere and featuring works which are perennial favourites. Outdoor concerts are also popular, where audiences can bring their own blankets and picnic baskets and feast under a twilight sky. The 'rules' that still exist are simply there to remind you to show the musicians and your fellow concert goers the respect they deserve.

Solo violinist Nigel Kennedy (b.1956) helped to popularize classical music with his flamboyant appearance.

## Tips for concert goers

- Be punctual. Most concert venues allow you in at a suitable break once the music has started. It is very distracting for musicians to see latecomers falling over their fellow patrons in an effort to get to their seats. If you are late, wait outside until you hear applause and then make a run for it.

Last Night of the Proms at the Royal Albert Hall, London, is a festive, rousing and usually informal affair.

- The fact that many concert halls are considering installing cellphone-jamming devices gives some indication of the frequency with which cellphones disrupt a performance. Leave your cellphone at home or switch it off before you take your seat. Similarly, silence beeping wristwatches and jangling jewellery.
- Casual dress is a safe option for most concerts, unless it is a gala performance or if you are someone's guest, in which case it is best to confirm the dress code beforehand.
- The changing nuances of classical music need a quiet audience to be fully appreciated. So hold back your comments until the clapping or the interval.
- If you have a cold or cough, bring along some cough lozenges and a supply of tissues. Unwrap the lozenges beforehand since the painfully slow unwrapping of a sweet will cause many a murderous stare from those around you. Also try and keep your coughing and sneezing to the noisy parts of the music.
- Sleeping during a performance is very bad manners. Even though you will not be sent to hell if you do, it's nice all the same if you respect the musicians enough to stay awake.
- If you are agonizing about when to clap, be aware that you are one of many. There will always be people in the audience who know when to put their hands together, so

There are few greater pleasures than watching an orchestra perform at night in the open air. It is a more relaxed occasion than a concert in a grand hall, but the rules of basic concert-going etiquette still apply

the golden rule is to wait and listen. Generally, do not applaud between movements. In a longer work, a brilliant performance will elicit spontaneous applause. If you are ecstatic, shout 'Bravo' for males and 'Brava' for females (the plural is 'Bravi').

- After a very good concert, applause and curtain calls can take a while, especially if the musicians indulge the audience with an encore. It is good manners to wait until the end before you leave the hall.
- Jazz concerts tend to be informal because they often take place in a club or restaurant, where it is quite acceptable to eat and even talk during a performance. But try not to make your voice heard above the music since your fellow patrons are entitled to hear the music.
- It is good manners, at a jazz concert, to clap after each number, even if you have to stop eating, but if a musician has just played a brilliant solo it is perfectly acceptable to clap during the piece.

Musicians are called to music like priests are called to the church. It is a calling that is not always possible to explain. They work relentlessly to master their art and it is the dream of every musician to receive the thankful applause after a concert well played – and a big, fat cheque, of course. The world would be a much poorer place if musicians ceased to exist because of the public was too apathetic to support them. Try to go to as many live concerts as possible, as this is truly the best way to listen to music as the composer intended it to be heard.

# LISTENING TO MUSIC AT HOME

Apart from the live concert, it is possible to listen to music almost anywhere. FM and satellite (digital) radio, as well as portable music players have given us the option of appreciating music while working, driving and even jogging. Technological advances have also made it possible to own a decent sound system without having to rob a bank.

The music you listen to will determine the kind of hi-fi system you choose. If you prefer classical music, you should invest in speakers which can handle the soft passages as well as the loud bits. There are many books and magazines on the subject of audio equipment, but here are a few useful things to bear in mind when you hit the shops.

- Take along a favourite CD so that you can 'test-drive' the various audio equipment on offer. This will make it easier for you to compare models and find the one that gives you the sound you want.
- Shop around, even for the same brand, because the price difference between various dealers can often be substantial. The Internet, audio catalogues and the Yellow Pages are good places to start your investigations.
- If you buy a brand you have never heard of, the chances are that customer service and repair may take a long time and cost a lot more than for an established brand which has built up a good reputation over the years.
- Remember that your living room has different proportions to that of the shop, which will change the sound of the system you buy. You may have to exchange your purchase a few times before you are satisfied, so buy from a dealer with a liberal return policy.
- The component that reads the information off a CD, mini-disc, etc, is the most important part of any audio set-up, so do not scrimp on this part of your system.
- If you listen to CDs only, it is pretty pointless to buy a tape deck. Fewer components mean you can allocate more money to each one. Additional components can be bought when the need arises.

## Buying pre-recorded music

Various considerations have to be taken into account, depending on the kind of music you buy. With pop music, either the artist or a particular song you like are the main concern. If you buy jazz, the name of the artist is paramount. When you buy classical music, you will usually be confronted with a number of recordings of the same work. Listen to them and decide which one you like best. As your musical taste develops, you will start preferring certain orchestras and soloists above others. However, don't be restrictive in your listening. Take a chance on some unknown names. You might just be pleasantly surprised.

## Building up your own recording collection

Musical taste is intensely personal and constantly evolves. We are not always in the same mood and this influences the kind of music we feel like listening to. There are many recorded works for violin (mostly classical) and it will take a while for you to establish your preferences. Luckily, the repertory is so varied it can become a hobby in itself to find your favourite composers, pieces and artists. To help you in your initial exploration I have included below a short list of some of the more popular works and violinists.

### LISTENING LIST

**Great Violinists** Affordable multi-volume series (Naxos)
**Jascha Heifetz** Tchaikovsky/Brahms *Violin Concertos* (RCA), *The Heifetz Collection* (many volumes) (RCA)
**Henryk Szeryng** Brahms/Khachaturian *Violin Concertos* (EMI), Bach *Partitas and Sonatas for Solo Violin* (Polygram)
**Yehudi Menuhin** Mendelssohn/Bruch *Violin Concertos* (EMI), Elgar *Violin Concerto* (EMI)
**David Oistrakh** Sibelius/Tchaikovsky *Violin Concertos* (EMI)
**Isaac Stern** *A Life in Music* (44 volumes) (Sony)
**Itzhak Perlman** Paganini *24 Caprices* (EMI), Brahms *Violin Sonatas* (EMI), *Side by Side* (Telarc)
**Tokyo String Quartet** Debussy/Ravel *String Quartets* (Sony), Schubert *Complete String Quartets* (Vox)
**Kyung Wha-Chung** Vivaldi *The Four Seasons* (EMI)
**Anne-Sophie Mutter** Beethoven *Violin Concerto* (DG)
**Arthur Grumiaux** Mozart *Violin Concertos* (Philips)
**Kennedy** *Plays Bach* (EMI), Elgar *Violin Concerto* (EMI)
**Joshua Bell** Bruch/Mendelssohn *Violin Concertos* (EMI)
**Maxim Vengerov** Prokofiev/Shostakovich *Violin Concertos* (Teldec), Schedrin/Stravinsky *Violin Concertos* (EMI)

**Other genres**
**Vanessa Mae** *The Best of Vanessa Mae* (EMI)
**The Chieftains** *Best of the Chieftains* (CBS)
**Jean-Luc Ponty** *Enigmatic Ocean* (Atlantic), *Jazz Violin Summit* (with Stephane Grappelli and Stuff Smith) (MPS)
**Stephane Grappelli** *Verve Jazz Masters* (Verve)

chapter six

# BUYING A VIOLIN & FINDING A TEACHER

AT SOME TIME OR ANOTHER IN YOUR MUSICAL MEANDERINGS, you will be confronted with the need to buy a violin and find a teacher to teach you how to play it – a dangerous situation financially and intellectually if you do not know what you are doing. Yet it is impossible to play without an instrument, and it is impossible to learn to play properly without a teacher.

The financial minefield that buying an instrument entails has put off many enthusiastic beginners. They have also often approached a teacher with great enthusiasm, only to leave him or her soon after, in a cloud of disillusionment, because the teacher did not understand their needs. Never fear. I and many other musicians have gone through the same problems and learned a thing or two which should benefit you.

The most important thing to do is to decide from the beginning what you want to achieve. Reading books like this one and asking knowledgeable people about music and the violin is a step in the right direction. Having some kind of goal in mind will help to make sure you do not waste too much time and money. Focus on which music you would like to play. Remember, however, that the violin is mostly considered a 'classical' instrument. Whether your preference lies with Mozart or Marilyn Manson, you will have to go through the same learning curve as every other violin student, and it is important to be patient, especially in the beginning. Just as you have to be very fit to run a marathon, you have to be able to play the notes before you can play your favourite music.

Apart from being patient, you also have to be shrewd when selecting an instrument and teacher. A bad instrument is not going to inspire you to play on it and a bad teacher is not going to inspire you to play at all. Remember your goal. It is the one thing that will propel you through any difficulties you may encounter. Also remember to enjoy your new pursuit. There is no use in doing something you don't enjoy. Music is there to be enjoyed, but it is also a barometer of your own personality. You will learn a great deal about yourself if you pursue music as a hobby or semi-professionally. Don't ever lose your initial enthusiasm.

**OPPOSITE:** Do not rush a purchase, as there are many aspects of buying a violin which should be considered carefully. Take an experienced violinist along with you to guide your decision.

## Buying a new violin

The only place to find a new violin is in a musical instrument shop, unless you happen to have a violin factory in your area. When inside the shop, you will usually be confronted with a wide selection of instruments. Violins will either be handcrafted or factory-made. Factory violins are cheaper, but a well-made violin by a master violin maker is usually of much higher quality. The first thing to do is get the right size. Since most violin beginners are children, there are variously sized violins to accommodate their growing bodies. Adults have the advantage of not having to switch from a violin of one size to another, but the only appropriate size for an adult (unless you have very, very small hands) is a full-size violin.

Next you have to choose a specific violin. Violin-makers often distinguish between student, orchestral and concert violins, but the names are less important than the price. Find the violins you can afford and then start experimenting with them. It is a good idea to take along a more experienced violinist. Apart from his or her opinion, you will have the added advantage of listening to the sound of the instrument from a distance. If you cannot find anyone to come with you, ask the owner or store assistant to demonstrate. A golden rule to remember is: a good violin will produce a stable, strong sound throughout its entire range.

After this, decide whether you prefer a violin with a more mellow sound or one with a bright, strident tone. When you have finally selected your violin (which could take some time), make sure you find out about the conditions of the sale. Ask the shop about insurance, payment options, guarantees and after-sale service.

Although most things are fixable, make sure you can afford to repair a second-hand instrument before you buy it.

Make sure your violin has a stable, strong sound throughout its tonal range.

## Buying a second-hand violin

Second-hand violins (or, in some cases, fiftieth-hand) are like an elusive prey to be carefully tracked down. They can be found in some unlikely places, like attics and antique shops. In addition, newspapers and the Yellow Pages also usually have sections devoted to second-hand instruments. It is also quite possible to hire second-hand instruments from music shops, music schools and private individuals.

A second-hand violin, other than a Stradivarius, is often a cheaper option and a good instrument for any beginner who may not keep his or her initial enthusiasm. However, the risk is usually much higher and you must scrutinize a second-hand instrument carefully to make sure it will not cost too much to get it in good working order. Although most things are fixable, check the instrument for worn varnish, strings and cracks.

Two problems which will be very expensive to fix include cracks near the bridge (and therefore the soundpost and bass-bar) and worn peg holes, which may require re-bushing or even necessitate replacing the entire pegbox.

If you do find a Stradivarius, however, any amount of fixing is worth it. It is worth having an experienced violinist with you when viewing a second-hand instrument, otherwise ask if you can have the violin appraised to make sure that you are not paying too much for it. Older is not necessarily better.

The last thing to bear in mind with any violin is that you must not be concerned if you sound bad on it. It will take some time before your playing will not inflict aural torture on innocent ears. A good player can get a surprisingly good sound, even out of a poor violin. Remember the joke: violin by Stradivarius; hands by Frankenstein.

## Caring for your violin

Once you have the violin safely at home, take proper care of it – it is an investment. If you want to upgrade later, you can use the money from the sale of your first violin for the purchase of your next one. Alternatively, you can collect violins and hire out the ones you aren't using to supplement your cash for a deposit on another one. Here are some tips:

- Depending on your financial status, get your violin serviced regularly by a professional. Once a year should be enough.
- Do not leave your violin lying around. This may seem obvious, but a violin is a very easy thing to fall over or sit on and then it will be useful only as a piece of modern sculpture. Put it back in its case after use and put the case somewhere out of the way, like the floor of the wardrobe.
- Rapid changes in temperature and humidity will adversely affect any wooden object. Give your violin a chance to acclimatize to a new environment inside its case before you take it out, to prevent the wood being affected.
- No food, especially fluid, should be brought near the instrument. It is also advisable to wash your hands before playing, because it minimizes the amount of dirt, sweat and dust you leave on the strings and fingerboard.
- After playing, wipe the body, strings and fingerboard with a soft dry cloth to remove dust, dirt and rosin.
- Never use household cleaners on a violin. Clean the fingerboard with a damp cloth and a small amount of methylated spirits (denatured alcohol), but do not bring the spirits anywhere near the varnish or body of the violin.
- After practice, loosen the ribbon of the bow before you pack it away. If a hair has broken, remove it by carefully breaking it off at either end of the bow.

## Buying violin accessories

When you start. it can be tempting to buy everything you see. Slow down. Buy what you need and then, if you can afford it, buy extras. Start with strings. There are three kinds of strings – synthetic, steel and gut. Each has its own advantages and disadvantages and their sounds also differ.

Synthetic strings are good to start on. They have a warm, mellow sound and, unlike gut, are not affected too much by temperature and humidity. Gut strings take a while to 'settle', so they may need constant retuning for the first day or two before you play them.

Steel strings have a bright, piercing sound and are perfect to play on from the start as they do not need to 'settle'.

There are two kinds of gut strings: uncovered and wound. Uncovered gut strings have a nasal quality and are prone to warp and break, but are perfect for early music since they give a subtle attack and have a long decay. If you use gut strings on a tailpiece with fine tuners, make sure they are the kind of fine tuners that will not break the strings.

Violin strings also come in various tensions and thicknesses, or gauges. The higher the tension, the louder the sound, but the higher stops are more difficult to play. The best advice is to experiment with different brands to find those you prefer.

Chin rests, shoulder rests, mutes and rosin come in various shapes and sizes. Choose rests that are comfortable for you. Experiment with the mute and types of rosin until you get the sound you want.

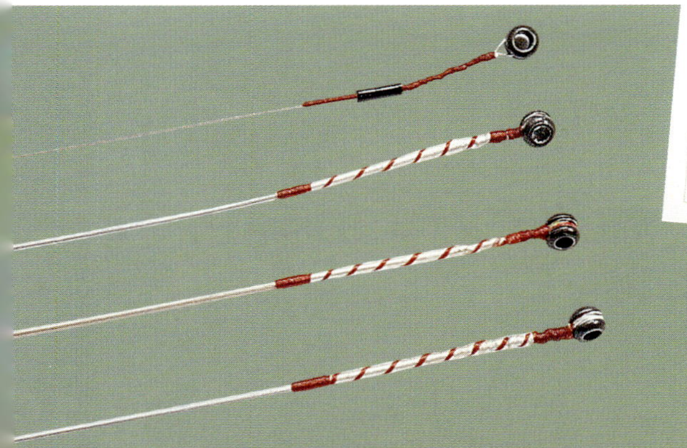

**ABOVE** Expensive strings can be purchased in tubes. Uncoiled strings have better tonal qualities. **RIGHT** Various international string brands.

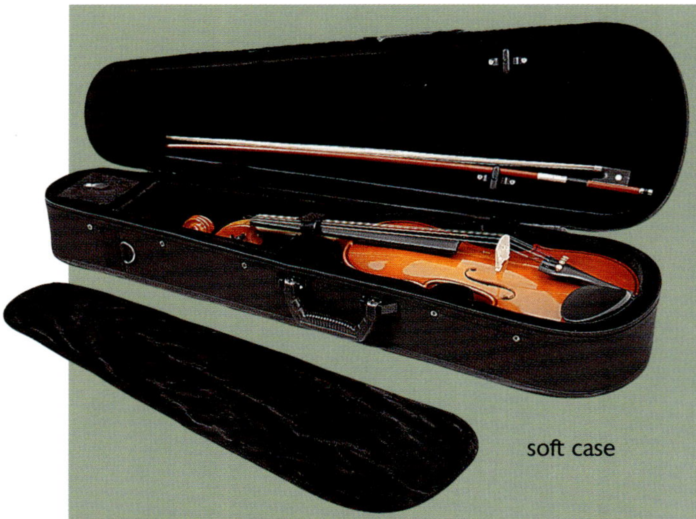


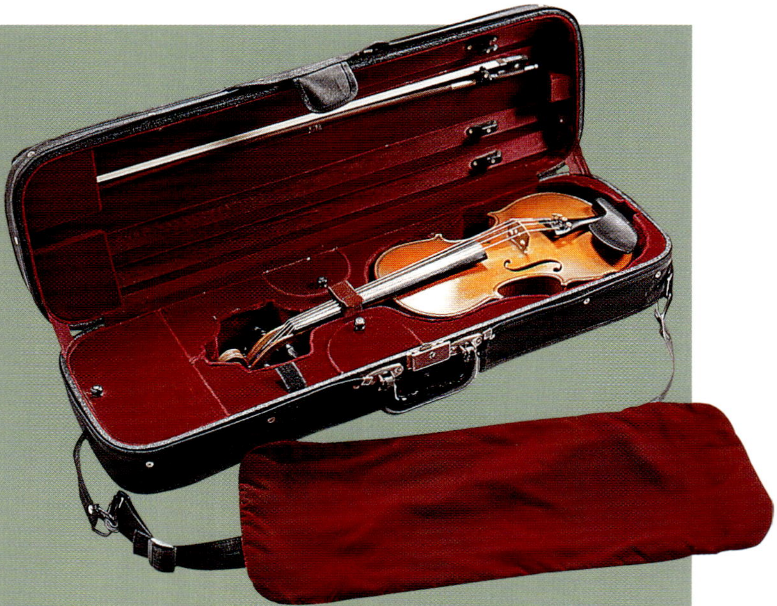


Violins can be stored in soft or hard cases. Soft cases are good for everyday use, but hard cases are essential if you travel a lot (especially on an airplane).

If you travel a lot and want to take your violin with you, a travel case or flight case (with a hard outer shell) is a good thing to have. For everyday use and over short distances, a soft padded case is better because it weighs less (you have to carry it around after all). Ask the dealer if your case is waterproof, but do not test it in your swimming pool.

Another accessory, which becomes necessary only if you go professional, is a second bow. To a professional player, a good bow is almost as essential as a good violin. But a good bow can be expensive. Most professional players have two or three different bows for the different styles of music they play.

If you have visions of becoming a Vanessa Mae (which will require you to be a talented drag queen if you are male), you can even buy a pickup and amplifier for your violin.

## Replacing strings

There are conflicting opinions about when you should change your strings. A rule of thumb is: replace your strings only when they break, have loose winding, are difficult to tune, or sound dull. Some strings last longer than others. A G string might last for a year, while a wound A string that is constantly played may only last for six weeks. If a new string sounds very different from the rest, you may have to replace the whole set.

Do not remove all the strings at once, since you need pressure on the bridge to keep it and the soundpost intact. Replace them two at a time, starting with one of the middle strings (because they go over the outer strings in the pegbox) and the outer string next to it.

Put the violin on a table or your lap with the scroll pointing away from you. Start by loosening the peg by turning it towards you (1), and then slowly remove the string from the peg. Be careful. If you pull out the entire string too fast, you could take out an eye. Now remove the other end of the string from the tailpiece (2).

Save old strings as emergency replacements by putting each string into the packet of the corresponding new string.

Take the new string and fit the correct end to the tailpiece. Stretch it over the correct groove in the bridge (3) and guide it over the fingerboard and through the correct groove in the nut. Remember to start with the outer string.

Now, keeping the string taut with your hand, pass the end of the string through the hole in the tuning peg and turn the peg away from you (4) until the string is secure. Repeat the process with the inner string as well.

When both strings are in place, tune them to the correct pitch by comparing their sound with the old strings (see p31). Now repeat the entire procedure with the other two strings.

It is always a good idea to get your teacher or somebody who is more experienced to help you change your strings the first few times.

## Buying sheet music

Sheet music refers to printed music. It can sometimes be bought in a shop selling instruments, or you can buy music from specialist sheet music shops, garage sales and private individuals. It helps to have a rough idea of the kind of music you are looking for. Here are a few things to bear in mind:

- Play from original sheet music. Playing from photocopies should be punishable by death, since it deprives many editors, typesetters, musicians and composers who are still alive of their rightful income.
- Look at the music and not just the cover. If the music looks too 'black' on first sight, goes higher than first position or has multiple stops, leave it until you are more confident about your playing abilities.
- If you are interested in the music of a specific composer or style, look for anthologies of music. They are usually graded in difficulty. If you want to play your favourite orchestral tunes, look for anthologies of orchestral excerpts for violin.
- Bear in mind that not all music is written for violin. If you want to play something written for another instrument, ask for a violin transcription or arrangement.
- Do not be restrictive in the music you buy. Take a chance on something you have never heard before. There is nothing better than discovering a beautiful piece of music by accident. It is also good for your sight-reading to play as many different pieces as possible.
- If the music you are looking for is not readily available, ask if it can be ordered for you. Remember that a handling fee (postage and packaging) could be charged.
- Buy an adjustable music stand so that you can play standing up or sitting down. It is also useful to have your own stand if you want to play with other musicians.
- When buying music for violin and accompaniment, ensure you obtain your own part and one for the accompanist. With chamber music, buy the score (which contains all the parts) and the individual part for each player.

## Taking lessons

It is advisable to take lessons from the beginning, since the violin is difficult to learn on your own. A good teacher will also make sure that incorrect playing does not become a habit. You can find teachers by contacting any local high schools, colleges or tertiary education institutions with a music faculty. Orchestras, arts councils and education authorities may also be able to give details concerning teachers in your area. Many orchestral players also teach to supplement their income. If you are not sure who to contact, speak to more experienced players and ask if they know of anyone who teaches violin.

- Contact the teacher and arrange an initial lesson. The first lesson establishes a rapport between teacher and student and you will be able to see if you are going to get along. Ask in advance about the cost of a trial lesson.

If music looks too 'black', as does the right-hand side of this Brandenburg Concerto facsimile, leave it until your playing improves.

Finding a good teacher is imperative to advancing your enjoyment and knowledge of playing the violin.

- Do not necessarily settle for the first teacher you find. You are going to be spending a lot of time and money and it is your right to find the best teacher for yourself. A good teacher is one who knows a lot about all aspects of music and is capable of inspiring you to do your best. He or she must also be able to meet your expectations and requirements at any given time.
- Ask about the teachers' qualifications and playing history. Performances and other musical activities should be taken into account, but many teachers have opted to teach from the start. Ask them why they are teaching. Do they enjoy it? Are they passionate about their instrument? Remember that just because a person passed an exam does not mean that he or she is going to motivate or inspire you or is even capable of playing well.
- Ask if you can contact the teacher if you have a problem. Beginners often require immediate responses and do not want to wait a whole week until their next lesson.
- If you are interested in chamber music or playing in a group, find a teacher who teaches a few instruments, so that you can be paired up with other students at the same level, or even join a beginner's orchestra.
- If you are changing teachers, ask the prospective teacher to listen to your playing so that he or she can compare their teaching style with that of your previous teacher.
- Remember that a violinist who has achieved performance recognition will probably charge much more per lesson than a full-time teacher.
- Once you have a playable violin and a decent teacher, the ball is in your court. The violin is a difficult instrument to master and you will progress beyond the basics only if you are willing to do regular technical, theoretical and sight-reading exercises. If you are hardworking and tenacious, the sky is the limit. Always remember to enjoy yourself.

**A tempo** If the tempo of a piece has changed, this signifies a return to the original tempo
**Alla breve** 2/2 time.
**Atonalism/Atonality** A system where no key is dominant. It came to the fore in the early 20th century and was pioneered by composers like Arnold Schoenberg.
**Calando** Decreasing in tempo and dynamic.
**Cantabile** In a singing style.
**Chord** The simultaneous sounding of a group of notes of different pitch.
**Clef** (French, 'key'.) A symbol at the beginning of a stave, fixing the pitch of notes according to their position on the stave.
**Counterpoint** Music that combines two or more individual melodic lines, or themes, to form a harmonious whole.
**Crescendo** (Italian, 'growing'.) Increasing in volume.
**Decrescendo** Decreasing in volume.
**Delicato** Delicately.
**Dissonance** Inharmonious; notes that 'clash' and do not agree with the harmony of a given chord.
**Dominant** In traditional tonality, the fifth tone of a scale.
**Dynamics** Variations in volume, from loud to soft. Dynamic marks or markings are the directions and symbols used to indicate degrees of loudness.
**Forte** (f), **fortissimo** (ff) (Italian. Loud and very loud.)
**Harmony** Any combination of notes that is sounded simultaneously in a way considered pleasant, in line with the concept of tonality and the major and minor keys.
**Interval** The difference of pitch between two notes, calculated by counting the steps on the diatonic scale between the two notes (e.g. the interval between C and G is a fifth).
**Key signature** The sharps or flats placed after the clef at the beginning of a stave to indicate the prevailing key.
**Largo** (Italian, 'broad'.) A slow and measured performance.
**Leading note** In traditional tonality, the note a semitone or tone below the first note of the scale.
**Legato** (Italian, 'bound together'.) A smooth performance.
**Mezzo** (Italian, 'half'.) Indicating moderately; hence mezzo forte (mf), between loud and soft.
**Note** A single musical sound (or tone) of specific pitch and duration. Any of a series of graphic signs representing a musical sound whose pitch is indicated by its position on the stave, and whose duration is indicated by the sign's shape.
**Opera** A dramatic work in which music forms the predominant part, consisting of arias (songs), recitatives (speech-song) and choruses, with elaborate and spectacular staging.
**Oratorio** An extended musical setting of a biblical or religious text for soloists, chorus and orchestra. Developed in Rome in the 17th century, it had a similar structure to an opera but was presented in a concert hall rather than acted out on a stage.
**Ornaments** Extra notes (e.g. trills, turns, etc.) added to vocal or instrumental melodies as a decoration or embellishment.
**Piano** (p), **pianissimo** (pp) (Italian. Quiet and very quiet.) To be played softly or very softly respectively.
**Pitch** The register ('highness' or 'lowness') of a note which determines its position on a stave; measured by the frequency of the vibrations that produce it.
**Poco** A little, e.g. poco ritardando, which means slowing down a little.
**Rallentando** (abbr. rall.) Alternative term for Ritardando.
**Rest** A measured silence.
**Rhythm** The organization of notes in a piece in relation to time. Rhythm is determined by the way the notes are grouped in bars, the number of beats in a bar, and the manner in which the beats are accented.
**Scale** A progression of notes, ascending or descending, by determined increments. There are various types of scale (e.g. chromatic, diatonic, major, minor, or twelve-note), depending on the musical system being used.
**Scordatura** Detuning the open strings to give unorthodox notes and tunings.
**Semitone** Half a tone; the smallest interval conventionally used in Western Classical music. (See also Interval.)
**Stave** or **staff** A grid of five parallel horizontal lines, and the corresponding spaces between them, on which notes are written. A note's position on the stave determines its relative pitch, with the point of reference indicated by the clef.
**Syncopation** An accent (or 'off-beat') placed on a normally unaccented beat of a bar (often the second or last beat), to achieve an irregular rhythm. A constant feature of jazz.
**Tempo** (Italian, 'time'.) The speed, or the pace, at which a piece is played.
**Tonalism/tonality** In composition, the basic principle of using a number of keys, one of which is predominant and provides the overall tonality of the music. Compare Atonalism.
**Multiple stopping** Playing on more than one string simultaneously; includes double-stopping (2 strings), triple-stopping (3 strings) and quadruple-stopping (4 strings).
**Triple time** Music with three beats to the bar, e.g. a waltz.
**Up-beat** The unaccented beat preceding the first accented beat of a the first bar.
**Vibrato** (Italian, 'vibrating'.) The technique of producing a warm sound by a slight but rapid change of pitch in a voice or instrument, creating a pulsating or throbbing effect.
**Virtuoso** A musical master with outstanding technical skill.

**PUBLISHER'S ACKNOWLEDGEMENTS**

The author and publisher thank Nicky Fransman, Ernest Meyer, Trevor van Rensburg, Denis Olivier and the staff of the Department of Music at the University of Stellenbosch for their assistance with the photographic shoot; the staff of the Music Library of the University, Beulah Gericke, Frida Bekker and Yusuf Ras, for their patience and infinite availability; Mr Heuer of Heuer Musikhaus, Stellenbosch for his kind indulgence; Violin lecturers Louis van der Watt and Susann Myrtens for their expertise; and models Wilken Calitz, Mareli la Grange, Carina du Toit, Anke Schwacher, Babette le Roux and Maja Plüddemann for their time. The author would like to thank Philip du Toit for his arrangement of the Gershwin piece and Tara Elliot for her astounding insight and inestimable assistance.

**PICTURE CREDITS**

**Bridgeman Art Library:** p55 (top left) *Christie's Images/ Private Collection.* **Caroline Jones:** p72 (top right). **Lebrecht Music Collection:** p10 (bottom left) – *AG*; p11 (top left) – *Colouriser AL*; pp82, 83 (top right) – *David Farrell*; pp26 (bottom), 27 – *Jim Four*; pp68, 74, 79, 80 – *Richard Haughton*; pp48 (bottom), 50, 52, 54, 55 (bottom left), 56, 58, 60, 61, 62, 64, 66 (top right), 66 (bottom left) – *Kate Mount.* **Redferns Music Library:** p76 – *James Fraher*; p70 – *Don Hunstein/Stagelimage*; p73 (top) – *Mick Hutson*; p11 (bottom right) – *Hayley Madden*; pp72 (bottom left), 73 – *David Redfern.* **Struik Image Library (SIL)** p84.

**USEFUL WEBSITES:**

*(The websites below were valid at the time of going to print. They offer a starting point for further investigation and no endorsement or recommendation on the part of the author or publisher should be inferred.)*

**andante.com** Weekly subscription newsletter providing the latest in classical music news, reviews and commentary.
**apassion4jazz.net** Styles, milestones, festivals and more.
**digitalviolin.com** A history of stringed instruments; famous violin makers and violinists, as well as playing techniques.
**juilliard.edu/about** The Juilliard School, New York.
**rcm.ac.uk** Royal College of Music, London.
**redhotjazz.com** Styles, artists, archives.
**rollingstone.com** Online site of the legendary magazine.
**strad.com** Appraisal of rare violins, restoration of old instruments, violins and violas offered for sale.
**violin-world.com** Comprehensive Australian site containing useful advice, articles, a directory of teachers, as well as free music lessons, classifieds and more.
**vsa.to/** Official website of The Violin Society of America.

**FURTHER READING:**

**Baker, Theodore**. *Baker's Biographical Dictionary of Musicians.* Revised by Nicholas Slonimsky. Shirmer Books, New York, 1992.

**Boyden, D.D**. *The History of Violin Playing from its Origins to 1761*. Oxford University Press (OUP). London, New York, Toronto, 1965.

**Cummings, David**. *Random House Encyclopedic Dictionary of Classical Music.*

**Fischer, S**. *300 exercises and practice routines for violin.* Peters. London, Frankfurt, Leipzig, New York, 1997.

**Flesch, C**. *The Art of Violin Playing.* Carl Fischer Inc. New York, 1930.

**Galamian, I**. *Principles of Violin Playing and Teaching.* Faber and Faber. London, 1970.

**Menuhin, Yehudi**. *Six Lessons with Yehudi Menuhin.* Faber Music Ltd. London, 1971.

**Rolland, P**. *Basic Principles of Violin Playing.* American String Teachers Association. Commemorative Edition, 1979.

**Sadie, Stanley** (ed.). *The New Grove Dictionary of Music and Musicians.* 2nd edition. Macmillan, 2001.
Online subscription version: www.grovemusic.com

**Sherman, R**. & **Seldon, P**. *The Complete Idiot's Guide to Classical Music.* Alpha Books (A Division of Macmillan Reference, USA), New York, 1997.

**Whone, H**. *The Simplicity of Playing the Violin.* Victor Gollancz Ltd. London, 1980.